THE
KYBALION
Study Guide

THE
KYBALION
Study Guide

*A Study of the Hermetic Philosophy
of Ancient Egypt and Greece*
Three Initiates

Introduction, Commentary, and Afterword
by Mitch Horowitz

Published 2020 by Gildan Media LLC
aka G&D Media
www.GandDmedia.com

FIRST EDITION 2020

Front cover design by David Rheinhardt of Pyrographx
Front cover art by Vince Rose

Interior design by Meghan Day Healey of Story Horse, LLC

Library of Congress Cataloging-in-Publication Data is available upon
request

ISBN: 978-1-7225-0164-8

10   9   8   7   6   5   4   3   2   1

To Hermes Trismegistus
known by the ancient Egyptians
as "the great great" and "master of masters"
this little volume of Hermetic Teachings
is reverently dedicated

"THE LIPS OF WISDOM ARE CLOSED, EXCEPT TO THE EARS OF UNDERSTANDING"

Contents

Introduction to the Study Guide

The Magic of The Kybalion
by Mitch Horowitz

I have a deep love for this book and for the Greek-Egyptian wisdom that underlies it.

Published in 1908, *The Kybalion* is both a book and a set of ideas that are easy to underestimate. It is tempting to describe *The Kybalion*, with its cryptic byline of "Three Initiates," as a novelty of early twentieth-century occultism. That is how I once saw it myself.

But I later realized that the book contains beautiful vestiges of ancient truths; truths that are centuries older, I think, than we have fully understood. I say that not in some fantastical or wishful fashion but with deep seriousness. In this study guide I am very specific about the historical antecedents of *The Kybalion*.

In a real sense, *The Kybalion* is a repository of thought that connects us, however tenuously and however the thread has thinned, frayed or broken, to esoteric ideas of the Ancient Egyptian past. Contemporary seekers really do have fragmentary connections to some of the esoteric philosophies of our ancestors. We are connected to some of the ancient seekers who realized that there is an extra-physical dimension to life; that life consists not only of harvesting crops, conducting commerce, making lists, and raising families, vital as those things are. But rather, as understood within traditions ranging from Egyptian to Taoist to Vedic, we are part of a scale of existence that is greater than physicality and cognition. This outlook is captured in the late-ancient Hermetic axiom, "as above, so below," which is at the heart *The Kybalion*.

It fills me with exuberance to seriously reconsider a book that has been surrounded by so much rumor and fantasy yet also possesses a serious core. Our era is over-eager to indulge in fantasies. People have all kinds of notions about conspiracies and deep states. These types of theories not only delude and blind people but, worst of all, cement an "us versus them" attitude. Yet for all the fantasizing and apocalyptic ruminations today we lose sight of real wonders. One of those wonders, as I alluded, is that we are not so separate from the experience of ancient wisdom seekers.

It is remarkable how wisdom will hide. Some of the primeval ideas to which I refer, which center on the mirroring of the psyche and the cosmos, are nestled within this short but epic volume, awaiting rediscovery.

Above all, I want this study guide to be practical. Hence, I am opening this volume by inviting you to do a small, private exercise. I'd like you to think of something that you deeply want in life. I want you to be very disclosing with yourself and very unembarrassed about whatever that something is. You do not have to reveal it to anyone. In fact, I advise not to.

It is not always easy to acknowledge our true desires to ourselves. I believe that one of the traps of our alternative spiritual culture is that we too often brandish terms like "nonattachment" or "identification" or "ego." We use these things almost like catechism to indicate what's right and wrong on the spiritual path. We're sometimes taught that our desires are illusory or *samsara*. Likewise, if we display a trait that we find unattractive in ourselves, we're apt to call it "personality;" and if we display a trait that we find appealing we may call it "essence." I'm unsure that any of these divisions—attachment/nonattachment, essence/personality, consciousness/ego, inner/outer—actually exist. They're just words around which we form a consensus. And in accepting them we often limit ourselves.

So, when I ask you to think of something you really want in life, it doesn't have to be something you consider spiritually sanctioned or acceptable to your peers. It just has to be honest. I encourage you to choose ethically. I believe that life is reciprocal and we honor this by doing nothing that would violate another person's search for his or her highest potential. That is my definition of ethics.

I ask you do to this exercise because it will place emotional drive at your back, which can direct and unleash tremendous energies. I hope that as you read this guide you will make connections and discover ways to apply some of the Hermetic ideas we'll explore to the cherished thing that you want. A passionate desire not only focuses the mind but also strengthens your ability to learn and practice.

I mentioned earlier that it is easy to dismiss a book like *The Kybalion*. At one time, based on a cursory reading, I concluded that the book contained some serviceable ideas from the New Thought tradition gussied up in the garb of Egyptian antiquity. I saw *The Kybalion* as an inspired piece of theater. I was turned off by its dramatic byline "Three Initiates."

I won't spend a great deal of time on this, but we know through documentation and historiography that the author of this book is, in fact, William Walker Atkinson (1862–1932), a prodigious New Thought writer, publisher, and philosopher in the early-twentieth century. Atkinson acknowledged his sole authorship in an entry in *Who's Who in America* in 1912. The book originally came from the Yogi Publication Society, which was Atkinson's publishing company in Chicago. Atkinson often wrote under pseudonyms. Three Initiates is his best known, but he also used Yogi Ramacharaka, Theron Q. Dumont, and Magus Incognito. He wrote many New Thought books under his own name, as well.

Rumors about the identity of the Three Initiates contributed to the book's allure. One of the most popular has Atkinson writing *The Kybalion* with American occultist Paul Foster Case (1884–1954). Case and Atkinson did, in fact, overlap living and working in Chicago. But at the time of the book's publication Case would have been 24 years old and he didn't begin producing his own literary efforts until about ten years later. It's unlikely that he was of the literary pedigree at that point to have been one of Atkinson's collaborators. Atkinson was enormously prolific and had no problem turning out about one hundred New Thought-themed books by the time of his death in California in 1932.

The authorship question settled, I considered *The Kybalion* a well-conceived variant of Atkinson's many projects in which he adapted ideas from New Thought, this time draped in Egyptian scenery. The book had some sound ideas, and that was that. But life throws you curveballs. And I got thrown a very strange curveball that returned me to *The Kybalion* with far greater estimation. It has since become one of the most important books in my life.

Urged on by a certain instinct, one summer I read the book five times consecutively. I became enthralled with it. I began to realize that *The Kybalion* had veritable connections to classical Hermeticism. I could see that the book contained genuine vestiges of what has reached us from Greek-Egyptian philosophy. I came to feel as though I was encountering it for the first time. Perhaps I was living out the book's dictum: "The lips of wisdom are closed, except to the ears of understanding."

I mentioned a curveball. I want to share the unadulterated story of how life returned me to *The Kybalion*. The spiritual teacher Jiddu Krishnamurti (1895–1986) observed that the greatest barrier to the individual search is the wish for respectability. Pursuing respectability stymies your questions and abilities. That observation has served as my north star. Because I come from a world, intellectually and professionally, where you are not supposed to take seriously books like *The Kybalion* or ideas from New Thought. The intellectual culture I grew up in associates seriousness with tradition, sanction, and scholasticism. I reject that. What connotes seriousness is the actual impact of an idea. The success of a philosophy is how it changes your conduct and experience of life.

"Does it work?" is the sole question I honor when approaching a philosophy. Everything else is negotiable. I obviously want to see that a philosophy is not violent, that it has ethical content, by which I mean it doesn't prohibit or block another individual from aspiring toward his or her full potential. If those considerations can be satisfied, and usually they can, then "Does it work?" is the one question I care about. In that vein, I want to tell you the story of how I returned to *The Kybalion*.

As I was researching my 2013 book *One Simple Idea*, a history of the New Thought movement, I made a delightful discovery. I found, to my astonishment, that a figure who some of you reading these words may have grown up watching, as I did, was a great admirer of this book—he was a dedicated and lifelong reader. I am speaking of the comedic actor Sherman Hemsley, who played George Jefferson on the long-running sit-com "The Jeffersons." I have a peculiar occult connection to the show. When I was in fifth grade, my classmates nicknamed me Mr. Bentley after George's British neighbor. (I can't imagine what they were thinking . . .) The actress Marla Gibbs, who played the maid Florence on "The Jeffersons" is actually very into Science of Mind, an important philosophy to me. I met Franklin Cover, the actor who played the neighbor Tom Willis on "The Jeffersons." He died in 2006 and his son Bradford Cover is a distinguished stage actor. I was at an off-Broadway show where Bradford was performing and a woman came up to Franklin and rudely asked him,

"What are you doing today?" He replied with such savoir-faire, "Well, nothing like this," complimenting his son. He was a true gentleman.

I was researching the history New Thought when I came upon this remarkable article from *TV Guide*, which was referred to me by Philip Deslippe, a wonderful scholar of metaphysical movements who has written extensively on *The Kybalion*. Philip shared a piece from 1982 when "The Jeffersons" was one of the hottest shows in the country. This was before the digital revolution, so to call a sitcom popular meant it went into millions of homes. Hemsley himself, who died in 2012, was a private figure and seldom granted interviews.

The February 6, 1982, issue featured a cover profile of the actor with the headline "Don't Ask How He Lives or What He Believes In: A Rare View of 'The Jeffersons' Star Who Works Hard to Hide an Unorthodox Lifestyle." In the piece, Hemsley obliquely credited a mysterious book and teacher with turning his life around as a young man. "Somewhere along the line," went the profile, "he met 'the man with the book'—although Sherman won't say which one. 'Don't want to advertise any book,' he grumbles. He is also very mysterious about exactly who the man was."

Hemsley's housemate, André Pavon, told *TV Guide* that the book was, in fact, *The Kybalion*. "He gave me that and others," Pavon said, adding, "It changed my life. He told me, 'You got to read it, man.'" Though sometimes depicted as a recluse, Hemsley simply lived by a different scale of values—those he derived from *The Kybalion* as well as his interests in meditation and Kabbalah. Asked why he didn't frequent Hollywood parties and restaurants, he replied: "Nothing goes on there. The most exciting things happen in the mind."

I was surprised to read all of this in what was then a mass, mainstream publication. Personally, I get attracted to ideas based on the figures behind them or associated with them. I thought to myself, this is a real-world example of a non-conforming man who achieved a pinnacle of success, and who felt that *The Kybalion* was a turning point in his life, even though he was reluctant to publicly discuss it. That touched something in me.

I decided to go back and the read the book again with fresh eyes, forgetting all judgments and everything that I thought I already knew. I did so, and I was ignited with excitement not only at the quality of the book's ideas but also their historical integrity.

This is where I want to say a word about the nature of Hermeticism, which is the late-ancient philosophy whose precepts animate *The Kybalion*. To understand *The Kybalion* requires understanding the development of the Hermetic literature upon which it is built.

In the decades immediately following the death of Christ, the City of Alexandria in Egypt was a crossroads of world culture. There was an intermingling of African, Far Eastern, Middle Eastern, Greek, Roman, even some

Indian cultures that met in Alexandria. It was a center of commerce, religion, and scholarship.

Egypt at that time had been subjugated by the Roman Empire. But the officials who acted as government administrators were Greek in nationality. They self identified, however, as Egyptian. Cleopatra (69–30 BC) was Greek but identified as Egyptian. She was a philo-Egyptian insofar as she revived Ancient Egyptian religion, temple orders, and cultic worship, all things that were flourishing in Alexandria in the decades following Christ. Many temple priests were themselves Egyptian but also spoke Greek.

The Greek administrative class intramarried to preserve its ruling bloodline but deeply identified with Egypt's religion, history, iconography, mythology, worship, and magic. The Greco-Egyptian literary class started to write down ancient Egyptian ideas and philosophies in the Greek language. Egypt's written language of hieroglyphs was heavily symbolic. Of course it had phonetic and expository qualities, but as a literary form it eluded easy understanding; this is true even in our own age when we expect that translation should open everything to us. But translation does not open everything. For generations, scholars and ministers read the King James Bible, taking certain meanings verbatim but more recent scholars compared Aramaic texts to Greek texts to Latin texts, and they realized that a lot had gotten lost. Debate persists over the meaning of certain terms and their context. You can imagine how much more difficult it is to grasp a language that isn't in a literary form of transmuted phonetics but consists of symbol and multiple meaning—each character containing layers.

The circle of Greek-Egyptian scribes used the more conventional (in the Western sense) letter-based, phonetically driven form of Greek. And they began transcribing some of the ancient teachings. Certain of these teachings did not actually exist in hieroglyphic form but were passed down in oral tradition, which was common in Eastern, Near Eastern, and African cultures.

Rather than signing their own names to these books of Egyptian magic, religion, and philosophy, the scribes favored another practice, which was also common in the ancient world: affixing the name of a venerated sage or god onto the manuscripts. This was seen as adding gravitas to a work of writing. And also because the manuscripts were seen as conveying sacred wisdom gleaned from perception of the larger world. The name that Greek-Egyptian scribes often fixed to these manuscripts was Hermes or Hermes Trismegistus, meaning thrice-greatest Hermes.

Hermes Trismegistus was a title of veneration the Greeks gave to Egypt's god of writing and intellect, Thoth. The Ancient Egyptians often depicted Thoth as an ibis-headed figure with the body of a man holding a writing stylus. The ibis was sacred to the ancients because as a water bird it occupied all spheres of existence: water, land, and air—and through flight the ibis was considered capable of transcending worlds. When the Greeks encountered the figure of Thoth, they regarded Egypt's god of intellect as so awesome a figure that they dubbed him thrice-greatest, or three-times greatest Hermes, pronouncing him three-times greater than their own god of communication, Hermes. In some lines of tradition, including later Renaissance thought, Hermes Trismegistus was considered a mythical sage who lived in the period of Abraham or Moses, a kind of progenitor to the prophets and patriarchs. The earliest record we have of the name Hermes Trismegistus is 172 B.C.

This is the philosophical and magical writing that became known as the Hermetic literature or *Hermetica*.

In the centuries following Christ, with the fall of Rome in the East and West, the advent of Christianity, and the later advent of Islam, Hermeticism and all the temple-based teachings fell into obscurity, oppression, and disuse. Surviving Hermetic manuscripts that were not destroyed were stowed in monasteries or spirited to other lands where they were sometimes translated into Arabic. Throughout the Dark Ages, however, the teachings were forgotten.

But with the flowering of the Italian Renaissance in Florence in the 1460s all of that began to change.

Within the Renaissance mindset there existed a great hunger to rediscover the ancient world. Many Renaissance scholars, translators, and philosophers believed that somewhere out there in the ruins of the ancient empires existed evidence of a *primeval theology*, which predated everything else and from which all the modern faiths grew. This was a driving passion of Renaissance thought.

Around 1462 a Byzantine monk entered court of the Florentine leader, Cosimo de Medici (1389–1464). The monk, who was probably in Cosimo's employ as an antiquities scout, had possession of a bundle of Greek manuscripts discovered somewhere in the Byzantine world. The tracts appeared to codify Ancient Egyptian religious, ethical and magical ideas. Their author: Hermes Trismegistus. Thus began the rediscovery of the Hermetic literature.

Cosimo was shocked and delighted with the find because he and his court scholars believed that this was evidence of the primeval theology. Eager to read this material before he died, the monarch directed one of his chief translators, Marsilio Ficino (1433–1499), to stop working on translations of Plato and instead direct his attention to the Hermetic literature. Ficino translated these manuscripts from Greek into Latin. In so doing, he created what is known today as the *Corpus Hermeticum*, a collection of Renaissance-era translations that comprise a key body of the Hermetic literature.

To the Renaissance mind, this Hermetic literature represented a wellspring of ideas that could antedate Moses, that could extend to the time of Abraham, and that spoke to the thirst for primeval theology—a theology thought to predate everything else. What appeared in this esoteric literature?

The central and most enduring theme of the Hermeticism is that the human mind is an extension and imitation of *Nous*, a Higher Mind that serves as the creative force behind all that is. Like the Higher Man, man can create within his own sphere.

This perspective finds particular expression in books I and XI of the seventeen tracts in the *Corpus Hermeticum*. In book I, sometimes called *The Divine Pymander of Hermes Trismegistus*, we learn of the mind as an extension of the higher: "... your mind is god the father; they are not divided from one another for their union is life." (Except where noted, I am quoting Brian P. Copenhaver's 1992 Cambridge University Press translation.) As we realize our creative capacities, book I teaches, we grow closer in nature to the Eternal: "... he who has understood himself advances toward god."

Book XI teaches that the awakened mind possesses not only powers of causation but bestows godlike status:

See what power you have, what quickness! If you can do these things, can god not do them? So you must think of god in this way, as having everything—the cosmos, himself, (the) universe—like thoughts within himself. Thus, unless you make yourself equal to god, you cannot understand god; like is understood by like. Make yourself grow to immeasurable immensity, out-

leap all body, outstrip all time, become eternity and you will understand god. Having conceived that nothing is impossible to you, consider yourself immortal and able to understand everything, all art, all learning, the temper of every living thing.

In the student-teacher dialogue called *Asclepius*, which is often grouped as a coda to the *Corpus Hermeticum*, man's estimate is further elevated. We first learn that "one who has joined himself to the gods in divine reverence, using the mind that joins him to the gods, almost attains divinity." Using a variant of the Hermetic formula, "as above, so below" (found in another text called *The Emerald Tablet*, to be discussed), this dialogue counsels: "Forms of all things follow kinds ... Thus, the kind made up of gods will produce from itself the forms of gods." This adds deeper resonance to man being made in God's image, as found in Hebrew scripture.

Hermes teaches his disciple Asclepius that man, at his highest, is on par with the gods: "Because of this, Asclepius, a human being is a great wonder, a living thing to be worshipped and honored: for he changes his nature into a god's ..."

Hermes ultimately evaluates man as even greater than the gods because while a god's nature is fixed in immorality, the striving and aware man is ever in process *of becoming and fulfilling* his highest nature: "In short, god made mankind good and capable of immortality through his two natures, divine and mortal, and so god willed the arrangement whereby mankind was ordained to be better than the gods, who were formed only from the immortal nature ..."

Moreover, man in his reverence and worship, performs necessary acts of caretaking of the gods: "He not only advances toward god; he also makes the gods strong."

The modern reader of Hermetic literature may find himself facing a question that also faces students of New Thought: given the causative powers ascribed to our minds, and the manner in which thought is said to relate to the highest source of creation, why do we suffer physical decline, illness, and bodily death? Indeed, the most Hermetic of all New Thought teachers, Neville Goddard (1905–1972), instructed that your mind is God, and all that you experience is the product of your imagination—so, again, why must we "die as princes?" as the psalmist puts it?

The *Corpus Hermetic* offers a reconciling response. Man, for all his potential greatness, is nonetheless conscripted to "cosmic framework" where physical laws must be suffered and limitations experienced. "The master of eternity," Hermes tells Asclepius, "is the first god, the world"—or great nature—"is second, mankind is the third." Man may be the greatest of beings in God's schema of creation, but he nonetheless remains bound to other aspects of the creative order.

In book I we hear: "mankind is affected by mortality because he is subject to fate"—fate being a term for nature's governance—"thus, although man is above the cosmic framework, he became a slave within in."

These views of man's greatness and weakness, the forces in which he functions, and his higher possibilities are considered with surprising adroitness in *The Kybalion*. In essence, *The Kybalion* adds specific techniques to the Hermetic principle that the individual mind is adjunct to the Mind of God, through which the individual may not only create but also aspire to his eventual return to the source of creation itself.

From these passages, you can begin to understand the excitement that Renaissance thinkers felt in the face of such ideas. But in generations ahead new complexities and considerations intervened.

In 1614, French-English scholar and linguist Isaac Casaubon published a critique of the *Corpus Hermeticum*. Through textual and language analysis, Casaubon demonstrated that the Hermetic writings did not belong to deepest antiquity, as many Renaissance scholars hoped, but rather were products of late-antiquity, written in the generations immediately following the death of Christ. Casaubon's readjusted timeline challenged and eventually dampened hopes that the Hermetic literature reflected humanity's earliest quest for meaning. Due to his findings, many later scholars and pedants came see the Hermetic literature as compromised and inauthentic. As the Renaissance gave way to the Age of Enlightenment, many scholars viewed the Hermetica somewhat in the same way that I once regarded *The Kybalion*: as artifice.

Seventeenth-century philosopher Sir Thomas Browne rejected this judgment and declared in response: "The severe Schools shall never laugh me out of the Philosophy of Hermes, that this visible World is but a Picture of the invisible wherein..." Browne was right: the critics' dismissals were grossly incomplete. Their summary judgment resulted in an underestimation and misappraisal of the Hermetica within the Western mind, and also left us with a paucity of quality English translations.

What the critics failed to appreciate was that, although the Hermetic literature was, in fact, produced in late antiquity the texts themselves were based upon an oral tradition whose roots extended to the much older reaches of Egyptian theology for which the Renaissance mind hungered. How do we know this? Because most of our ancient literature—Homer, Plato, Scripture, the Vedas, the Dhammapada, the Tao Te Ching—began in a form that predated written and symbolic language, and that was oral in nature. Most tradition, myths, ancient dramas, and ancient philosophy—as seen in the Socratic dialogues themselves—began in older spoken form. Based on consistency, there is no reason to suppose that the Hermetic literature was some kind of schismatic exception. That said, the *Corpus Hermeticum* also shows the influence of other, late-ancient influences, including Neo-Platonism, early Christianity, Gnosticism, and various Greek philosophical schools grouped together with Egyptian influences. It is no easy task to sort out where one influence begins and another ends. Like many classical and religious philosophies, it is a mosaic.

All deduction holds, and most scholars today agree,* that the Hermetica provides a core sample authentic of Egyptian tradition transcribed in Greek literary form. That, finally, is the historical value of the Hermetica: its teachings are a precious time capsule, which have reached us in expository language that we can understand.

As I was rereading *The Kybalion*, I identified a supple crisscrossing of correspondences between the thought in this book and the thought in Hermetic literature. That is why *The Kybalion* itself is a work of true value: it is a practical adaptation of Hermeticism.

In terms of sources, Atkinson was a capable surveyor of Victorian and Theosophically based translations of Hermetic literature, which is how the corpus was available to early twentieth-century readers. In particular, he would have encountered the translations of G.R.S. Mead (1863–1933), a scholar of ancient mysticism and one-time secretary to Madame H. P. Blavatsky (1831–1891), a figure whom Atkinson revered. The influence of Blavatsky's

---

* E.g., see *The Egyptian Hermes* by Garth Fowden (Princeton University Press, 1986, 1993.)

1888 occult opus *The Secret Doctrine* is evident at several points in Atkinson's writings, especially in the chapter on correspondences, where I think some of his depictions of spheres of existence grow excessive and dense.

Mead's three-volume 1906 translation of the Hermetica, *Thrice-Greatest Hermes*, published two years before *The Kybalion*, while thickly worded in late-Victorian prose, was then one of the few really valid sources of Hermetic ideas in English. With a skilled and discerning eye, Atkinson identified and distilled insights that corresponded to the sturdiest aspects of New Thought, or what William James had called "the religion of healthy-mindedness." Atkinson probably benefited from the work of a British occultist named Anna Kingsford and her writing partner Edward Maitland. They published a book on the ideas of Hermeticism in 1885, called *The Virgin of the World of Hermes Mercurius Trismegistus* (the title is based on another Hermetic text). Beyond a handful of Victorian translations of varying quality, there existed one English translation by English minister and scholar John Everard, published in 1650.

From this material, the seeker-writer used his considerable curatorial abilities and his own insights into the New Metaphysics to produce a marriage of ancient and modern psychological insights

The Kybalion is, above all, a practical work and its value must be finally measured in your lived experience, because its ideas are intended to be useful, impactful, and applicable.

Atkinson focused chiefly on the authentic Hermetic principle that Mind is the Great Creator. According to Hermetic literature, the supreme Mind or *Nous*, emanates through concentric spheres of existence; the intelligences inhabiting each sphere, including our own, possess like power to create, limited by the nature of their sphere. This echoes in *The Kybalion*. The work is also structured around "Seven Hermetic Principles," which follow from the Hermetic concept of "seven rulers" of nature. Man, we are told in book I of the *Corpus Hermeticum*, "had in himself all the energy of the rulers, who marveled at him, and each gave him a share of his own nature." (I quote from a 1977 translation by Far West Undertakings.)

Atkinson is particularly supple in adapting the Hermetic conception of gender, in which the masculine (conscious mind, in Atkinson's terms, and original man in the Hermetica) impregnates the feminine (subconscious mind to Atkinson, and nature in the Hermetica), to create the physical world.

Further still—and this is vital to the book's appeal for today's seeker—*The Kybalion* ably ventures a theory of mind causality. The book explains why, from the perspective of symbiotic hierarchy, our minds possess formative, creative abilities, and yet, even as we evince powers of causation, we are subject to limits of physicality and daily mechanics.

As articulated in Atkinson's chapter "'The All' in All," the individual may wield traits of a higher manifesting Force, but that does not make the individual synonymous with that Force. Man, the book counsels, may accomplish much within given parameters, including transcendence of commonly presumed limitations, influence over the minds of others, and co-creation of certain circumstances; but the book reminds the enthusiast that we bump against physical parameters even as we are granted the capacity to imitate the Power that set those parameters. In this, *The Kybalion* honors the views of the ancients.

Atkinson offers philosophical definitions of concepts of rhythm, polarity, paradox, compensation, and "Mental Gender." In a sense, the philosophy of *The Kybalion* is a modern amalgam of Hermeticism, Neo-Platonism, Transcendentalism, and New Thought. The book also attempts, however fitfully, to correspond its ideas to the early-twentieth century's nascent insights into quantum mechanics and the "new physics," which gained currency in the decades following its publication. In this sense, the author exaggerates only slightly when he writes: "We do not come expounding a new philosophy, but rather furnishing the outlines of a great world-old teaching which will make clear the teachings of others—which will serve as a Great Reconciler of differing theories, and opposing doctrines."

In scope and ambition, *The Kybalion* captured the mood and aspirations of the dawning New Age culture, which it also helped shape. The overall spirit of *The Kybalion* can be traced to book XI of the *Corpus Hermeticum*, in which Hermes (who here is not a god but a sage) is told by Supreme Mind that through the imagination he can discover the workings of Higher Creation: "If you do not make yourself equal to God you cannot understand Him. Like is understood by like." (I quote from the 1999 translation by Clement Salaman, et al, *The Way of Hermes*.) This echoes *The Emerald Tablet*'s principle "as above, so below." Hermes is told to use his mind to travel to all places, to unite opposites, to know all things, to transcend time and distance: "Become eternity and thus you will understand God. Suppose nothing to be impossible for yourself." Hermeticism teaches that we are granted a birthright of boundless creativity and expansion within the imagination. This teaching is central to Hermeticism and its modern re-sounding in *The Kybalion*.

For clarity, I must note that Hermeticism is not the religious ancestor to New Thought. The paucity of translations and the rural surroundings of most of America's New Thought pioneers in the mid-to-late nineteenth century placed these ideas off their path. Early New Thoughters were largely independent investigators who arrived at their insights about the mind's causative abilities chiefly through self-experiment, a topic I explore in *One Simple Idea: How Positive Thinking Reshaped Modern Life.*

But aspects of Hermeticism do represent a distant historical parallel to New Thought, especially Hermeticism's core idea that a Great Mind of Creation brought all things into being, and this same creative mental faculty dwells in all people, beings the Higher Mind created not only in its own image but to function in its likeness. In book I of the *Corpus Hermeticum* we are told: "... your mind is god the father; they are not divided from one another for their union is life." (I quote again from Copenhaver.) As we come to realize our creative capacities, the author reasons, we grow closer in nature and perspective to the Eternal: "... he who has understood himself advances toward god." This outlook is at home in nearly every New Thought book of the last century.

Were it somehow possible for contemporary seekers to reach back in time and have an exchange with the ancient Hermeticists, something like *The Kybalion* is probably as good an estimation as we can venture of what would appear.

We now turn to the text itself. You will find my commentary following each chapter (except for the final two, which review earlier material) and an afterword with self-study resources, a clarification of literary-historical terms, and an important final exercise.

I send you into this work with a salute from the last of the ancient Hermeticists, Greek writer Stobaeus who in 500 A.D. wrote: "Up, Up O ye gods! ... The dawn of a new day of justice invites us."

Introduction

———

We take great pleasure in presenting to the attention of students and investigators of the Secret Doctrines this little work based upon the world-old Hermetic Teachings. There has been so little written upon this subject, not withstanding the countless references to the Teachings in the many works upon occultism, that the many earnest searchers after the Arcane Truths will doubtless welcome the appearance of this present volume.

The purpose of this work is not the enunciation of any special philosophy or doctrine, but rather is to give to the students a statement of the Truth that will serve to reconcile the many bits of occult knowledge that they may have acquired, but which are apparently opposed to each other and which often serve to discourage and disgust the beginner in the study. Our intent is not to erect a new Temple of Knowledge, but rather to place in the hands of the student a Master-Key with which he may open the many inner doors in the Temple of Mystery through the main portals he has already entered.

There is no portion of the occult teachings possessed by the world which have been so closely guarded as the fragments of the Hermetic Teachings which have come down to us over the tens of centuries which have elapsed since the lifetime of its great founder, Hermes Trismegistus, the "scribe of the gods," who dwelt in old Egypt in the days when the present race of men was in its infancy. Contemporary with Abraham, and, if the legends be true, an instructor of that venerable sage, Hermes was, and is, the Great Central Sun of Occultism, whose rays have served to illumine the countless teachings which have been promulgated since his time. All the fundamental and basic teachings embedded in the esoteric teachings of every race may be traced back to Hermes. Even the most ancient teachings of India undoubtedly have their roots in the original Hermetic Teachings.

From the land of the Ganges many advanced occultists wandered to the land of Egypt, and sat at the feet of the Master. From him they obtained the Master-Key which explained and reconciled their divergent views, and thus the Secret Doctrine was firmly established. From other lands also came the learned ones, all of whom regarded Hermes as the Master of Masters, and his influ-

ence was so great that in spite of the many wanderings
from the path on the part of the centuries of teachers in
these different lands, there may still be found a certain
basic resemblance and correspondence which underlies
the many and often quite divergent theories entertained
and taught by the occultists of these different lands today.
The student of Comparative Religions will be able to perceive the influence of the Hermetic Teachings in every
religion worthy of the name, now known to man, whether
it be a dead religion or one in full vigor in our own times.
There is always certain correspondence in spite of the
contradictory features, and the Hermetic Teachings act
as the Great Reconciler.

The lifework of Hermes seems to have been in the
direction of planting the great Seed-Truth which has
grown and blossomed in so many strange forms, rather
than to establish a school of philosophy which would
dominate, the world's thought. But, nevertheless, the
original truths taught by him have been kept intact in
their original purity by a few men each age, who, refusing
great numbers of half-developed students and followers,
followed the Hermetic custom and reserved their truth
for the few who were ready to comprehend and master it. From lip to ear the truth has been handed down
among the few. There have always been a few Initiates in
each generation, in the various lands of the earth, who
kept alive the sacred flame of the Hermetic Teachings,
and such have always been willing to use their lamps to

re-light the lesser lamps of the outside world, when the light of truth grew dim, and clouded by reason of neglect, and when the wicks became clogged with foreign matter. There were always a few to tend faithfully the altar of the Truth, upon which was kept alight the Perpetual Lamp of Wisdom. These men devoted their lives to the labor of love which the poet has so well stated in his lines:

"O, let not the flame die out! Cherished age after age in its dark cavern—in its holy temples cherished. Fed by pure ministers of love—let not the flame die out!"

These men have never sought popular approval, nor numbers of followers. They are indifferent to these things, for they know how few there are in each generation who are ready for the truth, or who would recognize it if it were presented to them. They reserve the "strong meat for men," while others furnish the "milk for babes." They reserve their pearls of wisdom for the few elect, who recognize their value and who wear them in their crowns, instead of casting them before the materialistic vulgar swine, who would trample them in the mud and mix them with their disgusting mental food. But still these men have never forgotten or overlooked the original teachings of Hermes, regarding the passing on of the words of truth to those ready to receive it, which teaching is stated in The Kybalion as follows: "Where fall the footsteps of the Master, the ears of those ready for his Teaching open wide." And again: "When the ears of the student are ready to hear, then cometh the lips to fill them with wisdom." But their customary attitude has always been strictly in accordance with the other Hermetic aphorism, also in The Kybalion: "The lips of Wisdom are closed, except to the ears of Understanding."

There are those who have criticized this attitude of the Hermetists, and who have claimed that they did not manifest the proper spirit in their policy of seclusion and reticence. But a moment's glance back over the pages of history will show the wisdom of the Masters, who knew the folly of attempting to teach to the world that which it was neither ready or willing to receive. The Hermetists have never sought to be martyrs, and have, instead, sat silently aside with a pitying smile on their closed lips, while the "heathen raged noisily about them" in their customary amusement of putting to death and torture the honest but misguided enthusiasts who imagined that they could force upon a race of barbarians the truth capable of being understood only by the elect who had advanced along The Path.

And the spirit of persecution has not as yet died out in the land. There are certain Hermetic Teachings, which, if publicly promulgated, would bring down upon the teachers a great cry of scorn and revilement from the multitude, who would again raise the cry of "Crucify! Crucify."

In this little work we have endeavored to give you an idea of the fundamental teachings of The Kybalion, striving to give you the working Principles, leaving you to apply therm yourselves, rather than attempting to work out the teaching in detail. If you are a true student, you will be able to work out and apply these Principles—if not, then you must develop yourself into one, for otherwise the Hermetic Teachings will be as "words, words, words" to you.

THE THREE INITIATES.

COMMENTARY

Although Atkinson employs what I consider excessively dramatic language, he does get at points that have significant defense within modern scholarship.

Scholar Martin Bernal in *Black Athena* has penetratingly and convincingly argued for the underestimated influence of North African and Hermetic philosophy, particularly on Hellenic, Hebraic, Gnostic, and Christian thought. Scholar Frances Yates in *Giordano Bruno and the Hermetic Tradition* and other books has likewise argued for the vital and underappreciated links between Renaissance Hermeticism and the dawn of Enlightenment-era reason.

Atkinson's success at capturing ancient spiritual psychologies and highlighting ideas about mind, matter, and thought-creativity, some of which demonstrate authentic resonance with Hermetic antiquity, shows that *The Kybalion* is not modern New Thought clothed in ancient garb, as some critics posit; rather, the book serves as something close to what it claims to be: a "Great Reconciler" of metaphysical, transcendental, and esoteric philosophies. —MH

Chapter 1

The Hermetic Philosophy

"The lips of wisdom are closed, except to the ears of Understanding."

—THE KYBALION.

From old Egypt have come the fundamental esoteric and occult teachings which have so strongly influenced the philosophies of all races, nations and peoples, for several thousand years. Egypt, the home of the Pyramids and the Sphinx, was the birthplace of the Hidden Wisdom and Mystic Teachings. From her Secret Doctrine all nations have borrowed. India, Persia, Chaldea, Medea, China, Japan, Assyria, ancient Greece and Rome, and other ancient countries partook liberally at the feast of knowledge which the Hierophants and Masters of the Land of Isis so freely provided for those who came prepared to partake of the great store of Mystic and Occult Lore which the masterminds of that ancient land had gathered together.

In ancient Egypt dwelt the great Adepts and Masters who have never been surpassed, and who seldom have been equaled, during the centuries that have taken their processional flight since the days of the Great Hermes. In Egypt was located the Great Lodge of Lodges of the Mystics. At the doors of her Temples entered the Neophytes who afterward, as Hierophants, Adepts, and Masters, traveled to the four corners of the earth, carrying with them the precious knowledge which they were ready, anxious, and willing to pass on to those who were ready to receive the same. All students of the Occult recognize the debt that they owe to these venerable Masters of that ancient land.

But among these great Masters of Ancient Egypt there once dwelt one of whom Masters hailed as "The Master of Masters." This man, if "man" indeed he was, dwelt in Egypt in the earliest days. He was known as Hermes Trismegistus. He was the father of the Occult Wisdom; the founder of Astrology; the discoverer of Alchemy. The details of his life story are lost to history, owing to the lapse of the years, though several of the ancient countries disputed with each other in their claims to the honor of having furnished his birthplace—and this thousands of years ago. The date of his sojourn in Egypt, in that his last incarnation on this planet, is not now known, but it has been fixed at the early days of the oldest dynasties of

Egypt—long before the days of Moses. The best authorities regard him as a contemporary of Abraham, and some of the Jewish traditions go so far as to claim that Abraham acquired a portion of his mystic knowledge from Hermes himself.

As the years rolled by after his passing from this plane of life (tradition recording that he lived three hundred years in the flesh), the Egyptians deified Hermes, and made him one of their gods, under the name of Thoth. Years after, the people of Ancient Greece also made him one of their many gods—calling him "Hermes, the god of Wisdom." The Egyptians revered his memory for many centuries-yes, tens of centuries—calling him "the Scribe of the Gods," and bestowing upon him, distinctively, his ancient title, "Trismegistus," which means "the thrice-great"; "the great-great"; "the greatest-great"; etc. In all the ancient lands, the name of Hermes Trismegistus was revered, the name being synonymous with the "Fount of Wisdom."

Even to this day, we use the term "hermetic" in the sense of "secret"; "sealed so that nothing can escape"; etc., and this by reason of the fact that the followers of Hermes always observed the principle of secrecy in their teachings. They did not believe in "casting pearls before swine," but rather held to the teaching "milk for babes"; "meat for strong men," both of which maxims are familiar to readers of the Christian scriptures, but both of which had been used by the Egyptians for centuries before the Christian era.

And this policy of careful dissemination of the truth has always characterized the Hermetics, even unto the present day. The Hermetic Teachings are to be found in all lands, among all religions, but never identified with any particular country, nor with any particular religious sect. This because of the warning of the ancient teachers against allowing the Secret Doctrine to become crystallized into a creed. The wisdom of this caution is apparent to all students of history. The ancient occultism of India and Persia degenerated, and was largely lost, owing to the fact that the teachers became priests, and so mixed theology with the philosophy, the result being that the occultism of India and Persia has been gradually lost amidst the mass of religious superstition, cults, creeds and "gods." So it was with Ancient Greece and Rome. So it was with the Hermetic Teachings of the Gnostics and Early Christians, which were lost at the time of Constantine, whose iron hand smothered philosophy with the blanket of theology, losing to the Christian Church that which was its very essence and spirit, and causing it to grope throughout several centuries before it found the way back to its ancient faith, the indications apparent to all careful observers in this Twentieth Century being that the Church is now struggling to get back to its ancient mystic teachings.

But there were always a few faithful souls who kept alive the Flame, tending it carefully, and not allowing its light to become extinguished. And thanks to these staunch hearts, and fearless minds, we have the truth still with us. But it is not found in books, to any great extent. It has been passed along from Master to Student; from Initiate to Hierophant; from lip to ear. When it was written down at all, its meaning was veiled in terms of alchemy and astrology so that only those possessing the key could read it aright. This was made necessary in order to avoid the persecutions of the theologians of the Middle Ages, who fought the Secret Doctrine with fire and sword; stake, gibbet and cross. Even to this day there will be found but few reliable books on the Hermetic Philosophy, although there are countless references to it in many books written on various phases of Occultism. And yet, the Hermetic Philosophy is the only Master Key which will open all the doors of the Occult Teachings!

In the early days, there was a compilation of certain Basic Hermetic Doctrines, passed on from teacher to student, which was known as "THE KYBALION," the exact significance and meaning of the term having been lost for several centuries. This teaching, however, is known to many to whom it has descended, from mouth to ear, on and on throughout the centuries. Its precepts have never been written down, or printed, so far as we know. It was merely a collection of maxims, axioms, and precepts, which were non-understandable to outsiders, but which were readily understood by students, after the axioms, maxims, and precepts had been explained and exemplified by the Hermetic Initiates to their Neophytes. These teachings really constituted the basic principles of "The Art of Hermetic Alchemy," which, contrary to the general belief, dealt in the mastery of Mental Forces, rather than Material Elements—the Transmutation of one kind of Mental Vibrations into others, instead of the changing of one kind of metal into another. The legends of the "Philosopher's Stone" which would turn base metal into Gold, was an allegory relating to Hermetic Philosophy, readily understood by all students of true Hermeticism.

In this little book, of which this is the First Lesson, we invite our students to examine into the Hermetic Teachings, as set forth in THE KYBALION, and as explained by ourselves, humble students of the Teachings, who, while bearing the title of Initiates, are still students at the feet of HERMES, the Master. We herein give you many of the maxims, axioms and precepts of THE KYBALION, accompanied by explanations and illustrations which we deem likely to render the teachings more easily comprehended by the modern student, particularly as the original text is purposely veiled in obscure terms.

The original maxims, axioms, and precepts of THE KYBALION are printed herein, in italics, the proper credit being given. Our own work is printed in the regular way, in the body of the work. We trust that the many students to whom we now offer this little work will derive as much benefit from the study of its pages as have the many who have gone on before, treading the same Path to Mastery throughout the centuries that have passed since the times of HERMES TRISMEGISTUS—the Master of Masters—the Great-Great. In the words of "THE KYBALION":

> "*Where fall the footsteps of the Master, the ears of those ready for his Teaching open wide.*"
>
> —THE KYBALION.

> "*When the ears of the student are ready to hear, then cometh the lips to fill them with Wisdom.*"
>
> —THE KYBALION.

So that according to the Teachings, the passage of this book to those ready for the instruction will attract the attention of such as are prepared to receive the Teaching. And, likewise, when the pupil is ready to receive the truth, then will this little book come to him, or her. Such is The Law. The Hermetic Principle of Cause and Effect, in its aspect of The Law of Attraction, will bring lips and ear together—pupil and book in company. So mote it be!

COMMENTARY

The title *The Kybalion* has no exact meaning that anyone has been able to get at. My best sense is that it is a Hellenized version of *kabbalah*. (Kabbalah is never mentioned in the book.) In effect, Atkinson structures the book as a modern commentary on the unseen work *The Kybalion*, which is quoted only in aphorisms and passages. Hence, the reader never gets to experience the full or unmediated secret book named in the title, another mystery Atkinson that structured into the work.

—MH

Chapter 2

The Seven Hermetic Principles

"The Principles of Truth are Seven; he who knows these, understandingly, possesses the Magic Key before whose touch all the Doors of the Temple fly open."

—THE KYBALION.

The Seven Hermetic Principles, upon which the entire Hermetic Philosophy is based, are as follows:

1. The Principle of Mentalism.
2. The Principle of Correspondence.
3. The Principle of Vibration.
4. The Principle of Polarity.
5. The Principle of Rhythm.
6. The Principle of Cause and Effect.
7. The Principle of Gender.

These Seven Principles will be discussed and explained as we proceed with these lessons. A short explanation of each, however, may as well be given at this point.

1. The Principle of Mentalism

"The All is Mind; The Universe is Mental."
—THE KYBALION.

This Principle embodies the truth that "All is Mind." It explains that THE ALL (which is the Substantial Reality underlying all the outward manifestations and appearances which we know under the terms of "The Material Universe"; the "Phenomena of Life"; "Matter"; "Energy"; and, in short, all that is apparent to our material senses) is SPIRIT which in itself is UNKNOWABLE and UNDEFINABLE, but which may be considered and thought of as AN UNIVERSAL, INFINITE, LIVING MIND. It also explains that all the phenomenal world or universe is simply a Mental Creation of THE ALL, subject to the Laws of Created Things, and that the universe, as a whole, and in its parts or units, has its existence in the Mind of THE ALL, in which Mind we "live and move and have our being." This Principle, by establishing the Mental Nature of the Universe, easily explains all of the varied mental and psychic phenomena that occupy such a large portion of the public attention, and which, without such explanation, are non-understandable and defy scientific treatment. An understanding of this great Hermetic Principle of Mentalism enables the individual to readily grasp the laws of the Mental Universe, and to apply the same to his well-being and advancement. The Hermetic Student is enabled to apply intelligently the great Mental Laws, instead of using them in a haphazard manner. With the Master-Key in his possession, the student may unlock the many doors of the mental and psychic temple of knowledge, and enter the same freely and intelligently. This Principle explains the true nature of "Energy," "Power," and "Matter," and why and how all these are subordinate to the Mastery of Mind. One of the old Hermetic Masters wrote, long ages ago: "He who grasps the truth of the Mental Nature of the Universe is well advanced on The Path to Mastery." And these words are as true today as at the time they were first written. Without this Master-Key, Mastery is impossible, and the student knocks in vain at the many doors of The Temple.

2. The Principle of Correspondence

"As above, so below; as below, so above."
—THE KYBALION.

This Principle embodies the truth that there is always a Correspondence between the laws and phenomena of the various planes of Being and Life. The old Hermetic axiom ran in these words: "As above, so below; as below, so above." And the grasping of this Principle gives one the means of solving many a dark paradox, and hidden secret of Nature. There are planes beyond our knowing, but when we apply the Principle of Correspondence to them we are able to understand much that would otherwise be unknowable to us. This Principle is of universal application and manifestation, on the various planes of the material, mental, and spiritual universe—it is an Universal Law. The ancient Hermetists considered this Principle as one of the most important mental instruments by which man was able to pry aside the obstacles which hid from view the Unknown. Its use even tore aside the Veil of Isis to the extent that a glimpse of the face of the goddess might be caught. Just as a knowledge of the Principles of Geometry enables man to measure distant suns and their movements, while seated in his observatory, so a knowledge of the Principle of Correspondence enables Man to reason intelligently from the Known to the Unknown. Studying the monad, he understands the archangel.

3. The Principle of Vibration

"Nothing rests; everything moves; everything vibrates."
—THE KYBALION.

This Principle embodies the truth that "everything is in motion"; "everything vibrates"; "nothing is at rest"; facts which Modern Science endorses, and which each new scientific discovery tends to verify. And yet this Hermetic Principle was enunciated thousands of years ago, by the Masters of Ancient Egypt. This Principle explains that the differences between different manifestations of Matter, Energy, Mind, and even Spirit, result largely from varying rates of Vibration. From THE ALL, which is Pure Spirit, down to the grossest form of Matter, all is in vibration—the higher the vibration, the higher the position in the scale. The vibration of Spirit is at such an infinite rate of intensity and rapidity that it is practically at rest—just as a rapidly moving wheel seems to be motionless. And at the other end of the scale, there are gross forms of matter whose vibrations are so low as to seem at rest. Between these poles, there are millions upon millions of varying degrees of vibration. From corpuscle and electron, atom and molecule, to worlds and universes, everything is in vibratory motion. This is also true on the planes of energy and force (which are but varying degrees of vibration); and also on the mental planes (whose states depend upon vibrations); and even on to the spiritual planes. An understanding of this Principle, with the appropriate formulas, enables Hermetic students to control their own mental vibrations as well as those of others. The Masters also apply this Principle to the conquering of Natural phenomena, in various ways. "He who understands the Principle of Vibration, has grasped the scepter of power," says one of the old writers.

4. The Principle of Polarity

"Everything is Dual; everything has poles; everything has its pair of opposites; like and unlike are the same; opposites are identical in nature, but different in degree; extremes meet; all truths are but half-truths; all paradoxes may be reconciled."

—THE KYBALION.

This Principle embodies the truth that "everything is dual"; "everything has two poles"; "everything has its pair of opposites," all of which were old Hermetic axioms. It explains the old paradoxes, that have perplexed so many, which have been stated as follows: "Thesis and antithesis are identical in nature, but different in degree"; "opposites are the same, differing only in degree"; "the pairs of opposites may be reconciled"; "extremes meet"; "everything is and isn't, at the same time"; "all truths are but half-truths"; "every truth is half-false"; "there are two sides to everything," etc., etc., etc. It explains that in everything there are two poles, or opposite aspects, and that "opposites" are really only the two extremes of the same thing, with many varying degrees between them. To illustrate: Heat and Cold, although "opposites," are really the same thing, the differences consisting merely of degrees of the same thing. Look at your thermometer and see if you can discover where "heat" terminates and "cold" begins! There is no such thing as "absolute heat" or "absolute cold"—

the two terms "heat" and "cold" simply indicate varying degrees of the same thing, and that "same thing" which manifests as "heat" and "cold" is merely a form, variety, and rate of Vibration. So "heat" and "cold" are simply the "two poles" of that which we call "Heat"—and the phenomena attendant thereupon are manifestations of the Principle of Polarity. The same Principle manifests in the case of "Light and Darkness," which are the same thing, the difference consisting of varying degrees between the two poles of the phenomena. Where does "darkness" leave off, and "light" begin? What is the difference between "Large and Small"? Between "Hard and Soft"? Between "Black and White"? Between "Sharp and Dull"? Between "Noise and Quiet"? Between "High and Low"? Between "Positive and Negative"? The Principle of Polarity explains these paradoxes, and no other Principle can supersede it. The same Principle operates on the Mental Plane. Let us take a radical and extreme example—that of "Love and Hate," two mental states apparently totally different. And yet there are degrees of Hate and degrees of Love, and a middle point in which we use the terms "Like or Dislike," which shade into each other so gradually that sometimes we are at a loss to know whether we "like" or "dislike" or "neither." And all are simply degrees of the same thing, as you will see if you will but think a moment. And, more than this (and considered of more importance by the Hermetists), it is possible to change the vibrations of Hate to the vibrations of Love, in one's own mind, and in the minds of others. Many of you, who read these lines, have had personal experiences of the involuntary rapid transition from Love to Hate, and the reverse, in your own case and that of others. And you will therefore realize the possibility of this being accomplished by the use of the Will, by means of the Hermetic formulas. "Good and Evil" are but the poles of the same thing, and the Hermetist understands the art of transmuting Evil into Good, by means of an application of the Principle of Polarity. In short, the "Art of Polarization" becomes a phase of "Mental Alchemy" known and practiced by the ancient and modern Hermetic Masters. An understanding of the Principle will enable one to change his own Polarity, as well as that of others, if he will devote the time and study necessary to master the art.

5. The Principle of Rhythm

"Everything flows, out and in; everything has its tides; all things rise and fall; the pendulum-swing manifests in everything; the measure of the swing to the right is the measure of the swing to the left; rhythm compensates."
—THE KYBALION.

This Principle embodies the truth that in everything there is manifested a measured motion, to and fro; a flow and inflow; a swing backward and forward; a pendulum-like movement; a tide-like ebb and flow; a high-tide and low-tide; between the two poles which exist in accordance with the Principle of Polarity described a moment ago. There is always an action and a reaction; an advance and a retreat; a rising and a sinking. This is in the affairs of the Universe, suns, worlds, men, animals, mind, energy, and matter. This law is manifest in the creation and destruction of worlds; in the rise and fall of nations; in the life of all things; and finally in the mental states of Man (and it is with this latter that the Hermetists find the understanding of the Principle most important). The Hermetists have grasped this Principle, finding its universal application, and have also discovered certain means to overcome its effects in themselves by the use of the appropriate formulas and methods. They apply the Mental Law of Neutralization. They cannot annul the Principle, or cause it to cease its operation, but they have learned how to escape its effects upon themselves to a certain degree depending upon the Mastery of the Principle. They have learned how to use it, instead of being used by it. In this and similar methods, consist the Art of the Hermetists. The Master of Hermetics polarizes himself at the point at which he desires to rest, and then neutralizes the Rhythmic swing of the pendulum which would tend to carry him to the other pole. All individuals who have attained any degree of Self-Mastery do this to a certain degree, more or less unconsciously, but the Master does this consciously, and by the use of his Will, and attains a degree of Poise and Mental Firmness almost impossible of belief on the part of the masses who are swung backward and forward like a pendulum. This Principle and that of Polarity have been closely studied by the Hermetists, and the methods of counteracting, neutralizing, and using them form an important part of the Hermetic Mental Alchemy.

6. The Principle of Cause and Effect

"Every Cause has its Effect; every Effect has its Cause; everything happens according to Law; Chance is but a name for Law not recognized; there are many planes of causation, but nothing escapes the Law."

—THE KYBALION.

This Principle embodies the fact that there is a Cause for every Effect; an Effect from every Cause. It explains that: "Everything Happens according to Law"; that nothing ever "merely happens"; that there is no such thing as Chance; that while there are various planes of Cause and Effect, the higher dominating the lower planes, still nothing ever entirely escapes the Law. The Hermetists understand the art and methods of rising above the ordinary plane of Cause and Effect, to a certain degree, and by mentally rising to a higher plane they become Causers instead of Effects. The masses of people are carried along, obedient to environment; the wills and desires of others stronger than themselves; heredity; suggestion; and other outward causes moving them about like pawns on the

Chessboard of Life. But the Masters, rising to the plane above, dominate their moods, characters, qualities, and powers, as well as the environment surrounding them, and become Movers instead of pawns. They help to play the game of life, instead of being played and moved about by other wills and environment. They use the Principle instead of being its tools. The Masters obey the Causation of the higher planes, but they help to rule on their own plane. In this statement there is condensed a wealth of Hermetic knowledge—let him read who can.

7. The Principle of Gender

"Gender is in everything; everything has its Masculine and Feminine Principles; Gender manifests on all planes."
—THE KYBALION.

This Principle embodies the truth that there is GENDER manifested in everything—the Masculine and Feminine Principles ever at work. This is true not only of the Physical Plane, but of the Mental and even the Spiritual Planes. On the Physical Plane, the Principle manifests as SEX, on the higher planes it takes higher forms, but the Principle is ever the same. No creation, physical, mental or spiritual, is possible without this Principle. An understanding of its laws will throw light on many a subject that has perplexed the minds of men. The Principle of Gender works ever in the direction of generation, regeneration, and creation. Everything, and every person, contains the two Elements or Principles, or this great Principle, within it, him or her. Every Male thing has the Female Element also; every Female contains also the Male Principle. If you would understand the philosophy of Mental and Spiritual Creation, Generation, and Re-generation, you must understand and study this Hermetic Principle. It contains the solution of many mysteries of Life. We caution you that this Principle has no reference to the many base, pernicious and degrading lustful theories, teachings and practices, which are taught under fanciful titles, and which are a prostitution of the great natural principle of Gender. Such base revivals of the ancient infamous forms of Phallicism tend to ruin mind, body and soul, and the Hermetic Philosophy has ever sounded the warning note against these degraded teachings which tend toward lust, licentiousness, and perversion of Nature's principles. If you seek such teachings, you must go elsewhere for them—Hermeticism contains nothing for you along these lines. To the pure, all things are pure; to the base, all things are base.

COMMENTARY

This chapter is a very useful digest of the seven principles that are traced out in the remainder of the book. At times, when Atkinson's argument seems to grow discursive, I encourage you to refer back to this chapter (as I think the author intended) to stay grounded within the essential point he is making.

In this chapter, I'd like you to pay careful attention to three crucial principles, which are at the practical heart of *The Kybalion*: *correspondence*; *polarity*; and *rhythm*. These three laws trace out the arc of "as above, so below."

About the principle of correspondence, Atkinson writes:

> *Just as a knowledge of the Principles of Geometry enables man to measure distant suns and their movements, while seated in his observatory, so a knowledge of the Principle of Correspondence enables Man to reason intelligently from the Known to the Unknown. Studying the monad, he understands the archangel.*

It is a natural law that we can extrapolate from the micro to the macro, from the lowest to the highest. Would you like to know the reason for war? Search the violence within yourself. The dictum "know thyself," which we rarely follow to its full implications, allows us to understand the outer world.

About the principle of polarity, Atkinson writes:

> . . . all are simply degrees of the same thing, as you will see if you will but think a moment. And, more than this . . . it is possible to change the vibrations of Hate to the vibrations of Love, in one's own mind, and in the minds of others. Many of you, who read these lines, have had personal experiences of the involuntary rapid transition from Love to Hate, and the reverse, in your own case and that of others. And you will therefore realize the possibility of this being accomplished by the use of the Will, by means of the Hermetic formulas. "Good and Evil" are but the poles of the same thing, and the Hermetist understands the art of transmuting Evil into Good, by means of an application of the Principle of Polarity.

As explored later, we can, by concentrating on the opposing polarity of an emotion, mentally "shift" from one emotional state to its opposite. The key to this operation is accurately identifying the opposite state. Polarity is a universal law but it has particular application with regard to mood, emotion, mental state, and relationships.

About the principle of rhythm, Atkinson quotes *The Kybalion*: "rhythm compensates." That short phrase is of enormous importance. In a sense, it summarizes Ralph Waldo Emerson's 1841 essay "Compensation," which discusses the cyclical ebb and flow of life, and how every loss is naturally redressed.

The ever-changing nature of life does not mean that it lacks symmetry: the swing of a pendulum in one direction is mirrored by its swing to the other. Hence, when you are suffering an inevitable counter swing will provide respite. Moods and states are part of this lawful mirror-swing. Does this mean that good tidings must always be followed by bad? In the formula of *The Kybalion* (further explored in Chapter 11) you can elude the negative effects of rhythm by elevating your attention to a higher plane. The "swing" still occurs but does so on a lower psychological sphere. Atkinson puts it this way:

> *The Hermetists have grasped this Principle, finding its universal application, and have also discovered certain means to overcome its effects in themselves by the use of the appropriate formulas and methods. They apply the Mental Law of Neutralization. They cannot annul the Principle, or cause it to cease its operation, but they have learned how to escape its effects upon themselves to a certain degree depending upon the Mastery*

of the Principle. They have learned how to use it, instead of being used by it ... The Master of Hermetics polarizes himself at the point at which he desires to rest, and then neutralizes the Rhythmic swing of the pendulum which would tend to carry him to the other pole. All individuals who have attained any degree of Self-Mastery do this to a certain degree, more or less unconsciously, but the Master does this consciously, and by the use of his Will, and attains a degree of Poise and Mental Firmness almost impossible of belief on the part of the masses who are swung backward and forward like a pendulum.

Nor does a positive experience necessarily portend a negative one. Atkinson offers the proposition that a positive state is, in effect, "paid for" in advance by a prior negative state or occurrence. The negative swing, he writes, could also have occurred in a previous incarnation. You needn't worry about "paying up" to compensate for good tidings. You already have paid. The negative is precedent to the positive.

Finally, the keen reader will notice Atkinson's use of the phrase "GAME OF LIFE" under the principle of rhythm. This term reemerged as the title of Florence Scovel Shinn's enormously popular 1925 New Thought book, *The Game of Life and How to Play It*. Shinn spoke of her admiration for *The Kybalion*, particularly in *The Secret Door to Success* published in 1940, the year of her death. Neville Goddard also used the term "game of life."   —MH

Chapter 3

Mental Transmutation

"Mind (as well as metals and elements) may be transmuted, from state to state; degree to degree; condition to condition; pole to pole; vibration to vibration. True Hermetic Transmutation is a Mental Art."

—THE KYBALION.

As we have stated, the Hermetists were the original alchemists, astrologers, and psychologists, Hermes having been the founder of these schools of thought. From astrology has grown modern astronomy; from alchemy has grown modern chemistry; from the mystic psychology has grown the modern psychology of the schools. But it must not be supposed that the ancients were ignorant of that which the modern schools suppose to be their exclusive and special property. The records engraved on the stones of Ancient Egypt show conclusively that the ancients had a full comprehensive knowledge of astronomy, the very building of the Pyramids showing the connection between their design and the study of astronomical science. Nor were they ignorant of Chemistry, for the fragments of the ancient writings show that they were acquainted with the chemical properties of things; in fact, the ancient theories regarding physics are being slowly verified by the latest discoveries of modern science, notably those relating to the constitution of matter. Nor must it be supposed that they were ignorant of the so-called modern discoveries in psychology—on the contrary, the Egyptians were especially skilled in the science of Psychology, particularly in the branches that the modern schools ignore, but which, nevertheless, are being uncovered under the name of "psychic science" which is perplexing the psychologists of to-day, and making them reluctantly admit that "there may be something in it after all."

The truth is, that beneath the material chemistry, astronomy and psychology (that is, the psychology in its phase of "brain-action") the ancients possessed a knowledge of transcendental astronomy, called astrology; of transcendental chemistry, called alchemy; of transcendental psychology, called mystic psychology. They possessed the Inner Knowledge as well as the Outer Knowledge, the latter alone being possessed by modern scientists. Among the many secret branches of knowledge possessed by the Hermetists, was that known as Mental Transmutation, which forms the subject matter of this lesson.

"Transmutation" is a term usually employed to designate the ancient art of the transmutation of metals—particularly of the base metals into gold. The word "Transmute" means "to change from one nature, form, or substance, into another; to transform" (Webster). And accordingly, "Mental Transmutation" means the art of changing and transforming mental states, forms, and conditions, into others. So you may see that Mental Transmutation is the "Art of Mental Chemistry," if you like the term—a form of practical Mystic Psychology.

But this means far more than appears on the surface. Transmutation, Alchemy, or Chemistry on the Mental Plane is important enough in its effects, to be sure, and if the art stopped there it would still be one of the most important branches of study known to man. But this is only the beginning. Let us see why!

The first of the Seven Hermetic Principles is the Principle of Mentalism, the axiom of which is "THE ALL is Mind; the Universe is Mental," which means that the Underlying Reality of the Universe is Mind; and the Universe itself is Mental—that is, "existing in the Mind of THE ALL." We shall consider this Principle in succeeding lessons, but let us see the effect of the principle if it be assumed to be true.

If the Universe is Mental in its nature, then Mental Transmutation must be the art of CHANGING THE CONDITIONS OF THE UNIVERSE, along the lines of Matter, Force and mind. So you see, therefore, that Mental Transmutation is really the "Magic" of which the ancient; writers had so much to say in their mystical works, and about which they gave so few practical instructions. If All be Mental, then the art which enables one to transmute mental conditions must render the Master the controller of material conditions as well as those ordinarily called "mental."

As a matter of fact, none but advanced Mental Alchemists have been able to attain the degree of power necessary to control the grosser physical conditions, such as the control of the elements of Nature; the production or cessation of tempests; the production and cessation of earthquakes and other great physical phenomena. But that such men have existed, and do exist today, is a matter of earnest belief to all advanced occultists of all schools. That the Masters exist, and have these powers, the best teachers assure their students, having had experiences which justify them in such belief and statements. These Masters do not make public exhibitions of their powers, but seek seclusion from the crowds of men, in order to better work their may along the Path of Attainment. We mention their existence, at this point, merely to call your attention to the fact that their power is entirely Mental, and operates along the lines of the higher Mental Transmutation, under the Hermetic Principle of Mentalism. "The Universe is Mental"—The Kybalion.

But students and Hermetists of lesser degree than Masters—the Initiates and Teachers—are able to freely work along the Mental Plane, in Mental Transmutation. In fact all that we call "psychic phenomena"; "mental influence"; "mental science"; "new-thought phenomena," etc., operates along the same general lines, for there is but one principle involved, no matter by what name the phenomena be called.

The student and practitioner of Mental Transmutation works among the Mental Plane, transmuting mental conditions, states, etc., into others, according to various formulas, more or less efficacious. The various "treatments," "affirmations," "denials" etc., of the schools of mental science are but formulas, often quite imperfect and unscientific, of The Hermetic Art. The majority of modern practitioners are quite ignorant compared to the ancient masters, for they lack the fundamental knowledge upon which the work is based.

Not only may the mental states, etc., of one's self be changed or transmuted by Hermetic Methods; but also the states of others may be, and are, constantly transmuted in the same way, usually unconsciously, but often consciously by some understanding the laws and principles, in cases where the people affected are not informed of the principles of self-protection. And more than this, as many students and practitioners of modern mental science know, every material condition depending upon the minds of other people may be changed or transmuted in accordance with the earnest desire, will, and "treatments" of person desiring changed conditions of life. The public are so generally informed regarding these things at present, that we do not deem it necessary to mention the same at length, our purpose at this point being merely to show the Hermetic Principle and Art underlying all of these various forms of practice, good and evil, for the force can be used in opposite directions according to the Hermetic Principles of Polarity.

In this little book we shall state the basic principles of Mental Transmutation, that all who read may grasp the Underlying Principles, and thus possess the Master-Key that will unlock the many doors of the Principle of Polarity.

We shall now proceed to a consideration of the first of the Hermetic Seven Principles—the Principle of Mentalism, in which is explained the truth that "THE ALL is Mind; the Universe is Mental," in the words of The Kybalion. We ask the close attention, and careful study of this great Principle, on the part of our students, for it is really the Basic Principle of the whole Hermetic Philosophy, and of the Hermetic Art of Mental Transmutation.

COMMENTARY

In a sense, this chapter is a prelude to the consideration of the first Hermetic principle of the mental nature of the universe. Atkinson builds the argument for this principle across several of the following chapters.

This chapter clarifies that the methods in *The Kybalion* train the student chiefly in activities related to mind, emotion, intellect, and insight. This is a book of "mental alchemy"—the transmutation of moods, states, intuition, and (ethical) mental influence over others. Just as The All, or the Infinite Mind, creates on the cosmic scale so do our minds create—in the broadest sense—within the sphere we occupy.   —MH

Chapter 4

The All

"Under, and back of, the Universe of Time, Space and Change, is ever to be found The Substantial Reality—the Fundamental Truth."

—THE KYBALION.

"Substance" means: "that which underlies all outward manifestations; the essence; the essential reality; the thing in itself," etc. "Substantial" means: "actually existing; being the essential element; being real," etc. "Reality" means: "the state of being real; true, enduring; valid; fixed; permanent; actual," etc.

Under and behind all outward appearances or manifestations, there must always be a Substantial Reality. This is the Law. Man considering the Universe, of which he is a unit, sees nothing but change in matter, forces, and mental states. He sees that nothing really IS, but that everything is BECOMING and CHANGING. Nothing stands still—everything is being born, growing, dying— the very instant a thing reaches its height, it begins to decline—the law of rhythm is in constant operation— there is no reality, enduring quality, fixity, or substanti- ality in anything—nothing is permanent but Change. He sees all things evolving from other things, and resolving into other things—constant action and reaction; inflow and outflow; building up and tearing down; creation and destruction; birth, growth and death. Nothing endures but Change. And if he be a thinking man, he realizes that all of these changing things must be but outward appear- ances or manifestations of some Underlying Power— some Substantial Reality.

All thinkers, in all lands and in all times, have assumed the necessity for postulating the existence of this Sub- stantial Reality. All philosophies worthy of the name have been based upon this thought. Men have given to this Substantial Reality many names—some have called it by the term of Deity (under many titles). Others have called it "The Infinite and Eternal Energy" others have tried to call it "Matter"—but all have acknowledged its existence. It is self-evident it needs no argument.

In these lessons we have followed the example of some of the world's greatest thinkers, both ancient and modern—the Hermetic. Masters—and have called this Underlying Power—this Substantial Reality—by the Hermetic name of "THE ALL," which term we consider the most comprehensive of the many terms applied by Man to THAT which transcends names and terms.

We accept and teach the view of the great Hermetic thinkers of all times, as well as of those illumined souls who have reached higher planes of being, both of whom assert that the inner nature of THE ALL is UNKNOWABLE. This must be so, for naught by THE ALL itself can comprehend its own nature and being.

The Hermetists believe and teach that THE ALL, "in itself," is and must ever be UNKNOWABLE. They regard all the theories, guesses and speculations of the theologians and metaphysicians regarding the inner nature of THE ALL, as but the childish efforts of mortal minds to grasp the secret of the Infinite. Such efforts have always failed and will always fail, from the very nature of the task. One pursuing such inquiries travels around and around in the labyrinth of thought, until he is lost to all sane reasoning, action or conduct, and is utterly unfitted for the work of life. He is like the squirrel which frantically runs around and around the circling treadmill wheel of his cage, traveling ever and yet reaching nowhere—at the end a prisoner still, and standing just where he started.

And still more presumptuous are those who attempt to ascribe to THE ALL the personality, qualities, properties, characteristics and attributes of themselves, ascribing to THE ALL the human emotions, feelings, and characteristics, even down to the pettiest qualities of mankind, such as jealousy, susceptibility to flattery and praise, desire for offerings and worship, and all the other survivals from the days of the childhood of the race. Such ideas are not worthy of grown men and women, and are rapidly being discarded.

(At this point, it may be proper for me to state that we make a distinction between Religion and Theology—between Philosophy and Metaphysics. Religion, to us, means that intuitional realization of the existence of The All, and one's relationship to it; while Theology means the attempts of men to ascribe personality, qualities, and characteristics to it; their theories regarding its affairs, will, desires, plans, and designs, and their assumption of the office of "middle-men" between The All and the people. Philosophy, to us, means the inquiry after knowledge of things knowable and thinkable; while Metaphysics means the attempt to carry the inquiry over and beyond the boundaries and into regions unknowable and unthinkable, and with the same tendency as that of Theology. And consequently, both Religion and Philosophy mean to us things having roots in Reality, while Theology and Metaphysics seem like broken reeds, rooted in the quicksands of ignorance, and affording naught but the most insecure support for the mind or soul of Man. we do not insist upon our students accepting these definitions—we mention them merely to show our position. At any rate, you shall hear very little about Theology and Metaphysics in these lessons.)

But while the essential nature of THE ALL is Unknowable, there are certain truths connected with its existence which the human mind finds itself compelled to accept. And an examination of these reports form a proper subject of inquiry, particularly as they agree with the reports of the Illumined on higher planes. And to this inquiry we now invite you.

"THAT which is the Fundamental Truth—the Substantial Reality—is beyond true naming, but the Wise Men call it THE ALL." —THE KYBALION.

"In its Essence, THE ALL *is UNKNOWABLE."*
—THE KYBALION.

"But, the report of Reason must be hospitably received, and treated with respect." —THE KYBALION.

The human reason, whose reports we must accept so long as we think at all, informs us as follows regarding THE ALL, and that without attempting to remove the veil of the Unknowable:

(1) THE ALL must be ALL that REALLY IS. There can be nothing existing outside of THE ALL, else THE ALL would not be THE ALL.

(2) THE ALL must be INFINITE, for there is nothing else to define, confine, bound, limit; or restrict THE ALL. It must be Infinite in Time, or ETERNAL,—it must have

always continuously existed, for there is nothing else to have ever created it, and something can never evolve from nothing, and if it had ever "not been," even for a moment, it would not "be" now,—it must continuously exist forever, for there is nothing to destroy it, and it can never "not-be," even for a moment, because something can never become nothing. It must be Infinite in Space—it must be Everywhere, for there is no place outside of THE ALL—it cannot be otherwise than continuous in Space, without break, cessation, separation, or interruption, for there is nothing to break, separate, or interrupt its continuity, and nothing with which to "fill in the gaps." It must be Infinite in Power, or Absolute, for there is nothing to limit, restrict, restrain, confine, disturb or condition it—it is subject to no other Power, for there is no other Power.

(3) THE ALL must be IMMUTABLE, or not subject to change in its real nature, for there is nothing to work changes upon it nothing into which it could change, nor from which it could have changed. It cannot be added to nor subtracted from; increased nor diminished; nor become greater or lesser in any respect whatsoever. It must have always been, and must always remain, just what it is now—THE ALL—there has never been, is not now, and never will be, anything else into which it can change.

THE ALL being Infinite, Absolute, Eternal and Unchangeable it must follow that anything finite, changeable, fleeting, and conditioned cannot be THE ALL. And as there is Nothing outside of THE ALL, in Reality, then any and all such finite things must be as Nothing in Reality. Now do not become befogged, nor frightened—we are not trying to lead you into the Christian Science field under cover of Hermetic Philosophy. There is a Reconciliation of this apparently contradictory state of affairs. Be patient, we will reach it in time.

We see around us that which is called "Matter," which forms the physical foundation for all forms. Is THE ALL merely Matter? Not at all! Matter cannot manifest Life or Mind, and as Life and Mind are manifested in the Universe, THE ALL cannot be Matter, for nothing rises higher than its own source—nothing is ever manifested in an effect that is not in the cause—nothing is evolved as a consequent that is not involved as an antecedent. And then Modern Science informs us that there is really no such thing as Matter—that what we call Matter is merely "interrupted energy or force," that is, energy or force at a low rate of vibration. As a recent writer has said "Matter has melted into Mystery." Even Material Science has abandoned the theory of Matter, and now rests on the basis of "Energy."

Then is THE ALL mere Energy or Force? Not Energy or Force as the materialists use the terms, for their energy and force are blind, mechanical things, devoid of Life or Mind. Life and Mind can never evolve from blind Energy or Force, for the reason given a moment ago: "Nothing can rise higher than its source—nothing is evolved unless it is involved—nothing manifests in the effect, unless it is in the cause." And so THE ALL cannot be mere Energy or Force, for, if it were, then there would be no such things as Life and Mind in existence, and we know better than that, for we are Alive and using Mind to consider this very question, and so are those who claim that Energy or Force is Everything.

What is there then higher than Matter or Energy that we know to be existent in the Universe? LIFE AND MIND! Life and Mind in all their varying degrees of unfoldment! "Then," you ask, "do you mean to tell us that THE ALL is LIFE and MIND?" Yes! and No! is our answer. If you mean Life and Mind as we poor petty mortals know them, we say No! THE ALL is not that! "But what kind of Life and Mind do you mean?" you ask.

The answer is "LIVING MIND," as far above that which mortals know by those words, as Life and Mind are higher than mechanical forces, or matter—INFINITE LIVING MIND as compared to finite "Life and Mind." We mean that which the illumined souls mean when they reverently pronounce the word: "SPIRIT!"

"THE ALL" is Infinite Living Mind—the Illumined call it SPIRIT!

COMMENTARY

The first of the seven principles of *The Kybalion* is that *the universe is mental*. The supporting idea for that contention is, again, the Hermetic dictum, "as above, so below," found in *The Emerald Tablet*. This work is not often grouped with the traditional Hermetic literature because for many years it was considered a piece of pseudo-Hermetica created in the medieval era. But early twentieth-century scholars located Arabic versions of *The Emerald Tablet*, which date back to at least to the 700s or 800s AD. This suggests the existence of a still-earlier source because a great deal of original Hermetica got preserved not only in Greek but also later in Arabic. (For a useful historical analysis of *The Emerald Tablet* see *Meditations on the Tarot* by Anonymous aka Valentin Tomberg.)

One of the earliest English translations of *The Emerald Tablet* was by Isaac Newton (1642–1727), from which I quote the opening:

> *Tis true without lying, certain and most true.*
> *That which is below is like that which is above*
> *and that which is above is like that which is below*
> *to do the miracles of one only thing.*

The author of *The Kybalion* uses that reasoning as his jumping off point and goes into a rather extensive argument that circles back to it. In practical terms, the fact that you can picture things in your mind—worlds, possibilities, sensations, physicality—suggests that your creative and visualizing faculties mirror those of highest creation. The All, or ultimate substance, is *thought*. Thought is the one thing that we know as infinite, from which no part can be added or subtracted. Thought is The All. When we say "spiritual" we are assigning a phrase to thought in its highest source.

"As above, so below" means that our sphere of life is part of a series of concentric circles of creation—and whatever is experienced in one of those circles is necessarily experienced in the continuum of circles that extend to the ultimate source of mentality. Just as the The All creates via thought so do we create in our sphere.   —MH

Chapter 5

The Mental Universe

"The Universe is Mental—held in the Mind of THE ALL.*"*
—THE KYBALION.

THE ALL is SPIRIT! But what is Spirit? This question cannot be answered, for the reason that its definition is practically that of THE ALL, which cannot be explained or defined. Spirit is simply a name that men give to the highest conception of Infinite Living Mind—it means "the Real Essence"—it means Living Mind, as much superior to Life and Mind as we know them, as the latter are superior to mechanical Energy and Matter. Spirit transcends our understanding, and we use the term merely that we may think or speak of THE ALL. For the purposes of thought and understanding, we are justified in thinking of Spirit as Infinite Living Mind, at the same time acknowledging that we cannot fully understand it. We must either do this or stop thinking of the matter at all.

Let us now proceed to a consideration of the nature of the Universe, as a whole and in its parts. What is the Universe? We have seen that there can be nothing outside of THE ALL. Then is the Universe THE ALL? No, this cannot be, because the Universe seems to be made up of MANY, and is constantly changing, and in other ways it does not measure up to the ideas that we are compelled to accept regarding THE ALL, as stated in our last lesson. Then if the Universe be not THE ALL, then it must be Nothing—such is the inevitable conclusion of the mind at first thought. But this will not satisfy the question, for we are sensible of the existence of the Universe. Then if the Universe is neither THE ALL, nor Nothing, what Can it be? Let us examine this question.

If the Universe exists at all, or seems to exist, it must proceed in some way from THE ALL—it must be a creation of THE ALL. But as something can never come from nothing, from what could THE ALL have created it. Some philosophers have answered this question by saying that THE ALL created the Universe from ITSELF—that is, from the being and substance of THE ALL. But this will not do, for THE ALL cannot be subtracted from, nor divided, as we have seen, and then again if this be so, would not each particle in the Universe be aware of its being THE ALL— THE ALL could not lose its knowledge of itself, nor actually BECOME an atom, or blind force, or lowly living thing.

Some men, indeed, realizing that THE ALL is indeed ALL, and also recognizing that they, the men, existed, have jumped to the conclusion that they and THE ALL were identical, and they have filled the air with shouts of "I AM GOD," to the amusement of the multitude and the sorrow of sages. The claim of the corpuscle that: "I am Man!" would be modest in comparison.

But, what indeed is the Universe, if it be not THE ALL, not yet created by THE ALL having separated itself into fragments? What else can it be—of what else can it be made? This is the great question. Let us examine it carefully. We find here that the "Principle of Correspondence" (see Chapter 2.) comes to our aid here. The old Hermetic axiom, "As above so below," may be pressed into service at this point. Let us endeavor to get a glimpse of the workings on higher planes by examining those on our own. The Principle of Correspondence must apply to this as well as to other problems.

Let us see! On his own plane of being, how does Man create? Well, first, he may create by making something out of outside materials. But this will not do, for there are no materials outside of THE ALL with which it may create. Well, then, secondly, Man procreates or reproduces his kind by the process of begetting, which is self-multiplication accomplished by transferring a portion of his substance to his offspring. But this will not do, because THE ALL cannot transfer or subtract a portion of itself, nor can it reproduce or multiply itself—in the first place there would be a taking away, and in the second case a multiplication or addition to THE ALL, both thoughts being an absurdity. Is there no third way in which MAN creates? Yes, there is—he CREATES MENTALLY! And in so doing he uses no outside materials, nor does he reproduce himself, and yet his Spirit pervades the Mental Creation.

Following the Principle of Correspondence, we are justified in considering that THE ALL creates the Universe MENTALLY, in a manner akin to the process whereby Man creates Mental Images. And, here is where the report of Reason tallies precisely with the report of the Illumined, as shown by their teachings and writings. Such are the teachings of the Wise Men. Such was the Teaching of Hermes.

THE ALL can create in no other way except mentally, without either using material (and there is none to use), or else reproducing itself (which is also impossible). There is no escape from this conclusion of the Reason, which, as we have said, agrees with the highest teachings of the Illumined. Just as you, student, may create a Universe of your own in your mentality, so does THE ALL create Universes in its own Mentality. But your Universe is the mental creation of a Finite Mind, whereas that of THE ALL is the creation of an Infinite. The two are similar in kind, but infinitely different in degree. We shall examine more closely into the process of creation and manifestation as we proceed. But this is the point to fix in your minds at this stage: THE UNIVERSE, AND ALL IT CONTAINS, IS A MENTAL CREATION OF THE ALL. Verily indeed, ALL IS MIND!

"THE ALL creates in its Infinite Mind countless Universes, which exist for aeons of Time—and yet, to THE ALL, the creation, development, decline and death of a million Universes is as the time of the twinkling of an eye." —THE KYBALION.

"The Infinite Mind of THE ALL is the womb of Universes." —THE KYBALION.

The Principle of Gender (see Lesson I. and other lessons to follow) is manifested on all planes of life, material mental and spiritual. But, as we have said before, "Gender" does not mean "Sex" sex is merely a material manifestation of gender. "Gender" means "relating to generation or creation." And whenever anything is generated or created, on any plane, the Principle of Gender must be manifested. And this is true even in the creation of Universes.

Now do not jump to the conclusion that we are teaching that there is a male and female God, or Creator. That idea is merely a distortion of the ancient teachings on the subject. The true teaching is that THE ALL, in itself, is above Gender, as it is above every other Law, including those of Time and Space. It is the Law, from which the Laws proceed, and it is not subject to them. But when THE ALL manifests on the plane of generation or creation, then it acts according to Law and Principle, for it is moving on a lower plane of Being. And consequently it manifests the Principle of Gender, in its Masculine and Feminine aspects, on the Mental Plane, of course.

This idea may seem startling to some of you who hear it for the first time, but you have all really passively accepted it in your everyday conceptions. You speak of the Father-hood of God, and the Motherhood of Nature—of God, the Divine Father, and Nature the Universal Mother—and have thus instinctively acknowledged the Principle of Gender in the Universe. Is this not so?

But, the Hermetic teaching does not imply a real duality—THE ALL is ONE—the Two Aspects are merely aspects of manifestation. The teaching is that The Masculine Principle manifested by THE ALL stands, in a way, apart from the actual mental creation of the Universe. It projects its Will toward the Feminine Principle (which may be called "Nature") whereupon the latter begins the actual work of the evolution of the Universe, from simple "centers of activity" on to man, and then on and on still higher, all according to well-established and firmly enforced Laws of Nature. If you prefer the old figures of thought, you may think of the Masculine Principle as GOD, the Father, and of the Feminine Principle as NATURE, the Universal Mother, from whose womb all things have been born. This is more than a mere poetic figure of speech—it is an idea of the actual process of the creation of the Universe. But always remember, that THE ALL is but One, and that in its Infinite Mind the Universe is generated, created and exists.

It may help you to get the proper idea, if you will apply the Law of Correspondence to yourself, and your own mind. You know that the part of You which you call "I," in a sense, stands apart and witnesses the creation of mental Images in your own mind. The part of your mind in which the mental generation is accomplished may be called the "Me" in distinction from the "I" which stands apart and witnesses and examines the thoughts, ideas and images of the "Me." "As above, so below," remember, and the phenomena of one plane may be employed to solve the riddles of higher or lower planes.

Is it any wonder that You, the child, feel that instinctive reverence for THE ALL, which feeling we call "religion"—that respect, and reverence for THE FATHER MIND? Is it any wonder that, when you consider the works and wonders of Nature, you are overcome with a mighty feeling which has its roots away down in your inmost being? It is the MOTHER MIND that you are pressing close up to, like a babe to the breast.

Do not make the mistake of supposing that the little world you see around you—the Earth, which is a mere grain of dust in the Universe—is the Universe itself. There are millions upon millions of such worlds, and greater. And there are millions of millions of such Universes in existence within the Infinite Mind of THE ALL. And even in our own little solar system there are regions and planes of life far higher than ours, and beings compared to which we earth-bound mortals are as the slimy life-forms that dwell on the ocean's bed when compared to Man. There are beings with powers and attributes higher than Man has ever dreamed of the gods' possessing. And yet these beings were once as you, and still lower—and you will be even as they, and still higher, in time, for such is the Destiny of Man as reported by the Illumined.

And Death is not real, even in the Relative sense—it is but Birth to a new life—and You shall go on, and on, and on, to higher and still higher planes of life, for aeons upon aeons of time. The Universe is your home, and you shall explore its farthest recesses before the end of Time. You are dwelling in the Infinite Mind of THE ALL, and your possibilities and opportunities are infinite, both in time and space. And at the end of the Grand Cycle of Aeons, when THE ALL shall draw back into itself all of its creations—you will go gladly for you will then be able to know the Whole Truth of being At One with THE ALL. Such is the report of the Illumined—those who have advanced well along The Path.

And, in the meantime, rest calm and serene—you are safe and protected by the Infinite Power of the FATHER-MOTHER-MIND.

> "Within the Father-Mother Mind, mortal children are at home."   —THE KYBALION.

> "There is not one who is Fatherless, nor Motherless in the Universe."   —THE KYBALION.

COMMENTARY

Here and in the next chapter Atkinson seeks to iden-tify the possibilities that the seeker faces in his or her sphere of existence. The individual is not capable of functioning as the highest source of creation even though he reflects *its processes*. If one takes seriously the principle "as above, so below," restated in Scripture as "God created man in his own image," it follows that we are generative, creative beings albeit within our framework. We must discern those abilities—and their limits. We see this most sharply in matters of physical decline and mortality.

Some readers may wonder how this relates to the thought of Neville Goddard, a vital metaphysical thinker whom I professedly admire. Neville taught that your imagination is God, and he meant this in the most literal sense. That would seem at odds with some of what Atkinson writes in this chapter. But I am undis-turbed by the seeming opposition. One of the signs of spiritual and intellectual maturity is toleration of par-adox. Paradox is in the nature of ethical experiment. Life does not reveal itself in neatly stratified portions. I have long believed that Neville is right: mind is the ultimate arbiter of reality. But I have also written that we live under many laws and forces, or rather we expe-rience them. *The Kybalion* has helped me harmonize those points of view. We are connected to The All; and we advance in various incarnations toward The All; but we also participate in a life of physical parameters within the world that we are capable of experiencing. Our sensory experiences are necessarily limited. With those sensory limits come physical limits. Hence, the law of mind is modified by coexistent laws, just as the effects of gravity are modified by mass.   —MH

Chapter 6

The Divine Paradox

"The half-wise, recognizing the comparative unreality of the Universe, imagine that they may defy its Laws—such are vain and presumptuous fools, and they are broken against the rocks and torn asunder by the elements by reason of their folly. The truly wise, knowing the nature of the Universe, use Law against laws; the higher against the lower; and by the Art of Alchemy transmute that which is undesirable into that which is worthy, and thus triumph. Mastery consists not in abnormal dreams, visions and fantastic imaginings or living, but in using the higher forces against the lower—escaping the pains of the lower planes by vibrating on the higher. Transmutation, not presumptuous denial, is the weapon of the Master."

—The Kybalion.

This is the Paradox of the Universe, resulting from the Principle of Polarity which manifests when THE ALL begins to Create—hearken to it for it points the difference between half-wisdom and wisdom. While to THE INFINITE ALL, the Universe, its Laws, its Powers, its life, its Phenomena, are as things witnessed in the state of Meditation or Dream; yet to all that is Finite, the Universe must be treated as Real, and life, and action, and thought, must be based thereupon, accordingly, although with an ever understanding of the Higher Truth. Each according to its own Plane and Laws. Were THE ALL to imagine that the Universe were indeed Reality, then woe to the Universe, for there would be then no escape from lower to higher, divine ward—then would the Universe become a fixity and progress would become impossible. And if Man, owing to half-wisdom, acts and lives and thinks of the Universe as merely a dream (akin to his own finite dreams) then indeed does it so become for him, and like a sleep-walker he stumbles ever around and around in a circle, making no progress, and being forced into an awakening at last by his falling bruised and bleeding over the Natural Laws which he ignored. Keep your mind ever on the Star, but let your eyes watch over your footsteps, lest you fall into the mire by reason of your upward gaze. Remember the Divine Paradox, that while the Universe IS

NOT, still IT IS. Remember ever the Two Poles of Truth the Absolute and the Relative. Beware of Half-Truths.

What Hermetists know as "the Law of Paradox" is an aspect of the Principle of Polarity. The Hermetic writings are filled with references to the appearance of the Paradox in the consideration of the problems of Life and Being. The Teachers are constantly warning their students against the error of omitting the "other side" of any question. And their warnings are particularly directed to the problems of the Absolute and the Relative, which perplex all students of philosophy, and which cause so many to think and act contrary to what is generally known as "common sense." And we caution all students to be sure to grasp the Divine Paradox of the Absolute and Relative, lest they become entangled in the mire of the Half-Truth. With this in view this particular lesson has been written. Read it carefully!

The first thought that comes to the thinking man after he realizes the truth that the Universe is a Mental Creation of THE ALL, is that the Universe and all that it contains is a mère illusion; an unreality; against which idea his instincts revolt. But this, like all other great truths, must be considered both from the Absolute and the Relative points of view. From the Absolute viewpoint, of course, the Universe is in the nature of an illusion, a dream, a phantasmagoria, as compared to THE ALL in itself. We recognize this even in our ordinary view, for we speak of the world as "a fleeting show" that comes and goes, is born and dies—for the element of impermanence and change, finiteness and unsubstantiality, must ever be connected with the idea of a created Universe when it is contrasted with the idea of THE ALL, no matter what may be our beliefs concerning the nature of both. Philosopher, metaphysician, scientist and theologian all agree upon this idea, and the thought is found in all forms of philosophical thought and religious conceptions, as well as in the theories of the respective schools of metaphysics and theology.

So, the Hermetic Teachings do not preach the unsubstantiality of the Universe in any stronger terms than those more familiar to you, although their presentation of the subject may seem somewhat more startling. Anything that has a beginning and an ending must be, in a sense, unreal and untrue, and the Universe comes under the rule, in all schools of thought. From the Absolute point of view, there is nothing Real except THE ALL, no matter what terms we may use in thinking of, or discussing the subject. Whether the Universe be created of Matter, or whether it be a Mental Creation in the Mind of THE ALL—it is unsubstantial, non-enduring, a thing of time, space and change. We want you to realize this fact thoroughly, before you pass judgment on the Hermetic conception of the Mental nature of the Universe. Think over any and all of the other conceptions, and see whether this be not true of them.

But the Absolute point of view shows merely one side of the picture—the other side is the Relative one. Absolute Truth has been defined as "Things as the mind of God knows them," while Relative Truth is "Things as the highest reason of Man understands them." And so while to THE ALL the Universe must be unreal and illusionary, a mere dream or result of meditation, nevertheless, to the finite minds forming a part of that Universe, and viewing it through mortal faculties, the Universe is very real indeed, and must be so considered. In recognizing the Absolute view, we must not make the mistake of ignoring or denying the facts and phenomena of the Universe as they present themselves to our mortal faculties—we are not THE ALL, remember.

To take familiar illustrations, we all recognize the fact that matter "exists" to our senses—we will fare badly if we do not. And yet, even our finite minds understand the scientific dictum that there is no such thing as Matter from a scientific point of view—that which we call Matter is held to be merely an aggregation of atoms, which atoms themselves are merely a grouping of units of force, called electrons or "ions," vibrating and in constant circular motion. We kick a stone and we feel the impact—it seems to be real, notwithstanding that we know it to be merely what we have stated above. But remember that our foot, which feels the impact by means of our brains, is likewise Matter, so constituted of electrons, and for that matter so are our brains. And, at the best, if it were not by reason of our Mind, we would not know the foot or stone at all.

Then again, the ideal of the artist or sculptor, which he is endeavoring to reproduce in stone or on canvas, seems very real to him. So do the characters in the mind of the author; or dramatist, which he seeks to express so that others may recognize them. And if this be true in the case of our finite minds, what must be the degree of Reality in the Mental Images created in the Mind of the Infinite? Oh, friends, to mortals this Universe of Mentality is very real indeed—it is the only one we can ever know, though we rise from plane to plane, higher and higher in it. To know it otherwise, but actual experience, we must be THE ALL itself. It is true that the higher we rise in the scale—the nearer to "the mind of the Father" we reach—the more apparent becomes the illusory nature of finite things, but not until THE ALL finally withdraws us into itself does the vision actually vanish.

So, we need not dwell upon the feature of illusion. Rather let us, recognizing the real nature of the Universe, seek to understand its mental laws, and endeavor to use them to the best effect in our upward progress through life, as we travel from plane to plane of being. The Laws of the Universe are none the less "Iron Laws" because of the mental nature. All, except THE ALL, are bound by them. What is IN THE INFINITE MIND OF THE ALL is REAL in a degree second only to that Reality itself which is vested in the nature of THE ALL.

So, do not feel insecure or afraid—we are all HELD FIRMLY IN THE INFINITE MIND OF THE ALL, and there is naught to hurt us or for us to fear. There is no Power outside of THE ALL to affect us. So we may rest calm and secure. There is a world of comfort and security in this realization when once attained. Then "calm and peaceful do we sleep, rocked in the Cradle of the Deep"—resting safely on the bosom of the Ocean of Infinite Mind, which is THE ALL. In THE ALL, indeed, do "we live and move and have our being."

Matter is none the less Matter to us, while we dwell on the plane of Matter, although we know it to be merely an aggregation of "electrons," or particles of Force, vibrating rapidly and gyrating around each other in the formations of atoms; the atoms in turn vibrating and gyrating, forming molecules, which latter in turn form larger masses of Matter. Nor does Matter become less Matter, when we follow the inquiry still further, and learn from the Hermetic Teachings, that the "Force" of which the electrons are but units is merely a manifestation of the Mind of THE ALL, and like all else in the Universe is purely Mental in its nature. While on the Plane of matter, we must recognize its phenomena—we may control Matter (as all Masters of higher or lesser degree do), but we do so by applying the higher forces. We commit a folly when we attempt to deny the existence of Matter in the relative aspect. We may deny its mastery over us—and rightly so—but we should not attempt to ignore it in its relative aspect, at least so long as we dwell upon its plane.

Nor do the Laws of Nature become less constant or effective, when we know them, likewise, to be merely mental creations. They are in full effect on the various planes. We overcome the lower laws, by applying still higher ones—and in this way only. But we cannot escape Law or rise above it entirely. Nothing but THE ALL can escape Law—and that because THE ALL is LAW itself, from which all Laws emerge. The most advanced Masters may acquire the powers usually attributed to the gods of men; and there are countless ranks of being, in the great hierarchy of life, whose being and power transcends even that of the highest Masters among men to a degree unthinkable by mortals, but even the highest Master, and the highest Being, must bow to the Law, and be as Nothing in the eye of THE ALL. So that if even these highest Beings, whose powers exceed even those attributed by men to their gods—if even these are bound by and are subservient to Law, then imagine the presumption of mortal man, of our race and grade, when he dares to consider the Laws of Nature as "unreal!" visionary and illusory, because he happens to be able to grasp the truth that the Laws are Mental in nature, and simply Mental Creations of THE ALL. Those Laws which THE ALL intends to be governing Laws are not to be defied or argued away. So long as the Universe endures, will they endure—for the Universe exists by virtue of these Laws which form its framework and which hold it together.

The Hermetic Principle of Mentalism, while explaining the true nature of the Universe upon the principle that all is Mental, does not change the scientific conceptions of the Universe, Life, or Evolution. In fact, science merely corroborates the Hermetic Teachings. The latter merely teaches that the nature of the Universe is "Mental," while modern science has taught that it is "Material"; or (of late) that it is "Energy" at the last analysis. The Hermetic Teachings have no fault to find with Herbert Spencer's basic principle which postulates the existence of an "Infinite and Eternal Energy, from which all things proceed." In fact, the Hermetics recognize in Spencer's philosophy the highest outside statement of the workings of the Natural Laws that have ever been promulgated, and they believe Spencer to have been a reincarnation of an ancient philosopher who dwelt in ancient Egypt thousands of years ago, and who later incarnated as Heraclitus, the Grecian philosopher who lived B.C. 500. And they regard his statement of the "Infinite and Eternal Energy" as directly in the line of the Hermetic Teachings, always with the addition of their own doctrine that his "Energy" is the Energy of the Mind of THE ALL. With the Master-Key of the Hermetic Philosophy, the student of Spencer will be able to unlock many doors of the inner philosophical conceptions of the great English philosopher, whose work shows the results of the preparation of his previous incarnations. His teachings regarding Evolution and Rhythm are in almost perfect agreement with the Hermetic Teachings regarding the Principle of Rhythm.

So, the student of Hermetics need not lay aside any of his cherished scientific views regarding the Universe.

All he is asked to do is to grasp the underlying principle of "THE ALL is Mind; the Universe is Mental—held in the mind of THE ALL." He will find that the other six of the Seven Principles will "fit into" his scientific knowledge, and will serve to bring out obscure points and to throw light in dark corners. This is not to be wondered at, when we realize the influence of the Hermetic thought of the early philosophers of Greece, upon whose foundations of thought the theories of modern science largely rest. The acceptance of the First Hermetic Principle (Mentalism) is the only great point of difference between Modern Science and Hermetic students, and Science is gradually moving toward the Hermetic position in its groping in the dark for a way out of the Labyrinth into which it has wandered in its search for Reality.

The purpose of this lesson is to impress upon the minds of our students the fact that, to all intents and purposes, the Universe and its laws, and its phenomena, are just as REAL, so far as Man is concerned, as they would be under the hypotheses of Materialism or Energism. Under any hypothesis the Universe in its outer aspect is changing, ever-flowing, and transitory—and therefore devoid of substantiality and reality. But (note the other pole of the truth) under the same hypotheses, we are compelled to ACT AND LIVE as if the fleeting things were real and substantial. With this difference, always, between the various hypotheses—that under the old views Mental Power was ignored as a Natural Force, while under Mentalism it becomes the Greatest Natural Force. And this one difference revolutionizes Life, to those who understand the Principle and its resulting laws and practice.

So, finally, students all, grasp the advantage of Mentalism, and learn to know, use and apply the laws resulting therefrom. But do not yield to the temptation which, as The Kybalion states, overcomes the half-wise and which causes them to be hypnotized by the apparent unreality of things, the consequence being that they wander about like dream-people dwelling in a world of dreams, ignoring the practical work and life of man, the end being that "they are broken against the rocks and torn asunder by the elements, by reason of their folly." Rather follow the example of the wise, which the same authority states, "use Law against Laws; the higher against the lower; and by the Art of Alchemy transmute that which is undesirable into that which is worthy, and thus triumph." Following the authority, let us avoid the half-wisdom (which is folly) which ignores the truth that: "Mastery consists not in abnormal dreams, visions, and fantastic imaginings or living, but in using the higher forces against the lower—escaping the pains of the lower planes by vibrating on the higher." Remember always, student, that "Transmutation, not presumptuous denial, is the weapon of the Master." The above quotations are from The Kybalion, and are worthy of being committed to memory by the student.

We do not live in a world of dreams, but in an Universe which while relative, is real so far as our lives and actions are concerned. Our business in the Universe is not to deny its existence, but to LIVE, using the Laws to rise from lower to higher—living on, doing the best that we can under the circumstances arising each day, and living, so far as is possible, to our biggest ideas and ideals. The true Meaning of Life is not known to men on this plane— if, indeed, to any—but the highest authorities, and our own intuitions, teach us that we will make no mistake in living up to the best that is in us, so far as is possible, and realising the Universal tendency in the same direction in spite of apparent evidence to the contrary. We are all on The Path—and the road leads upward ever, with frequent resting places.

Read the message of The Kybalion—and follow the example of "the wise"—avoiding the mistake of "the half-wise" who perish by reason of their folly.

COMMENTARY

I was asked this question by reader Josh T. Romero, which may shed light on some of the ideas in this section: "According *The Kybalion*, Matter and Spirit are opposite ends of polarity, so if you can polarize states at will . . . what does it look like to attain spirit?" I wrote back:

"That is a hugely well-timed question since I was literally just assembling commentary to the corresponding chapter *The Divine Paradox*. While Spirit and Matter may be polarities on the scale of the universe, we must function, most of the time, within the polarities that govern our plane of existence. We do not have access to Spirit in its ultimate form—we are much closer on the scale of existence to the coarsest forms of matter, and we must contend with the limits of our framework. This idea is also found in the thought of spiritual teacher G.I. Gurdjieff.

"We can, through intensive work, begin to glean and experience realities that exist on a higher scale than the one we occupy. This might appear to us, for example, in forms of psychical ability where we begin to experience the extra-physical nature of thought. Although these experiences are provably real (see *The Miracle Club*) they are not always repeatable."

Part of the value of *The Kybalion* is that the book does something that New Thought's pioneers never really did: consider the potential limitation or disadvantages of man's place in creation. The British judge Thomas Troward, a key New Thought intellect, surmised in a series of 1904 lectures that man is the pinnacle of evolutionary creation. As such, Troward reasoned, man possesses access to the "ultimate principle of intelligence," with which he serves as a co-creator. The flaw in Troward's approach is that he did not question man's apex; he did not consider that a ladder of creation may extend far beyond man in an unimaginable cosmic scheme in which man plays no part.

Troward and his closest followers did not consider the possibility that man possesses limited perspective, and is a being whose existence may be relative to some higher intelligence just as a plant is relative to man. Man is neither all-seeing or all-knowing; and his creative faculties, whatever their nature, cannot surpass his point of perspective.

Ralph Waldo Emerson sought to resolve this problem. He took account of both aspects of human existence—man's great potential and unthinkable smallness—in his 1860 essay, "Fate." Emerson wrote, "But the soul contains the event that shall befall it; for the event is only the actualization of its thoughts, and what we pray to ourselves for is always granted." Yet Emerson also insisted that man's creative faculties are not all that he lives under. He added that there is just "one key, one solution to the mysteries of human condition." And that is to acknowledge that man exists under both self-direction and nature's will. And the will of nature contains purposes we cannot know, but can only bow to, and thus take our place in creation. "So when a man is victim of his fate," Emerson continued, ". . . he is to rally on his relation to the Universe, which his ruin benefits. Leaving the daemon who suffers, he is to take sides with the Deity who secures universal benefit by his pain."   —MH

Chapter 7

"The All" In All

"While All is in The All, it is equally true that The All is in All. To him who truly understands this truth hath come great knowledge."

—THE KYBALION.

How often have the majority of people heard repeated the statement that their Deity (called by many names) was "All in All" and how little have they suspected the inner occult truth concealed by these carelessly uttered words? The commonly used expression is a survival of the ancient Hermetic Maxim quoted above. As the Kybalion says: "To him who truly understands this truth, hath come great knowledge." And, this being so, let us seek this truth, the understanding of which means so much. In this statement of truth—this Hermetic Maxim—is concealed one of the greatest philosophical, scientific and religious truths.

We have given you the Hermetic Teaching regarding the Mental Nature of the Universe—the truth that "the Universe is Mental—held in the Mind of THE ALL." As the Kybalion says, in the passage quoted above: "All is in THE ALL." But note also the co-related statement, that: "It is equally true that THE ALL is in ALL." This apparently contradictory statement is reconcilable under the Law of Paradox. It is, moreover, an exact Hermetic statement of the relations existing between THE ALL and its Mental Universe. We have seen how "All is in THE ALL"—now let us examine the other aspect of the subject.

The Hermetic Teachings are to the effect that THE ALL is Imminent in ("remaining within; inherent; abiding within") its Universe, and in every part, particle, unit, or combination, within the Universe. This statement is usually illustrated by the Teachers by a reference to the Principle of Correspondence. The Teacher instructs the student to form a Mental Image of something, a person, an idea, something having a mental form, the favorite example being that of the author or dramatist forming an idea of his characters; or a painter or sculptor forming an image of an ideal that he wishes to express by his art. In each case, the student will find that while the image has its existence, and being, solely within his own mind, yet he, the student, author, dramatist, painter, or sculptor, is, in a sense, immanent in; remaining within; or abiding within, the mental image also. In other words, the entire virtue, life, spirit, of reality in the mental image is derived from the "immanent mind" of the thinker. Consider this for a moment, until the idea is grasped.

To take a modern example, let us say that Othello, Iago, Hamlet, Lear, Richard III, existed merely in the mind of Shakespeare, at the time of their conception or creation. And yet, Shakespeare also existed within each of these characters, giving them their vitality, spirit, and action. Whose is the "spirit" of the characters that we know as Micawber, Oliver Twist, Uriah Heep—is it Dickens, or have each of these characters a personal spirit, independent of their creator? Have the Venus of Medici, the Sistine Madonna, the Apollo Belvidere, spirits and reality of their own, or do they represent the spiritual and mental power of their creators? The Law of Paradox explains that both propositions are true, viewed from the proper viewpoints. Micawber is both Micawber, and yet Dickens. And, again, while Micawber may be said to be Dickens, yet Dickens is not identical with Micawber. Man, like Micawber, may exclaim: "The Spirit of my Creator is inherent within me—and yet I am not HE!" How different this from the shocking half-truth so vociferously announced by certain of the half-wise, who fill the air with their raucous cries of: "I am God!" Imagine poor Micawber, or the sneaky Uriah Heep, crying: "I Am Dickens"; or some of the lowly clods in one of Shakespeare's plays, eloquently announcing that: "I Am Shakespeare!" THE ALL is in the earthworm, and yet the earth-worm is far from being THE ALL. And still the wonder remains, that though the earth-worm exists merely as a lowly thing, created and having its being solely within the Mind of THE ALL—yet THE ALL is immanent in the earthworm, and in the particles that go to make up the earth-worm. Can there be any greater mystery than this of "All in THE ALL; and THE ALL in All?"

The student will, of course, realize that the illustrations given above are necessarily imperfect and inadequate, for they represent the creation of mental images in finite minds, while the Universe is a creation of Infinite Mind—and the difference between the two poles separates them. And yet it is merely a matter of degree—the same Principle is in operation—the Principle of Correspondence manifests in each—"As above, so Below; as Below, so above."

And, in the degree that Man realizes the existence of the Indwelling Spirit immanent within his being, so will he rise in the spiritual scale of life. This is what spiritual development means—the recognition, realization, and manifestation of the Spirit within us. Try to remember this last definition—that of spiritual development. It contains the Truth of True Religion.

There are many planes of Being—many sub-planes of Life—many degrees of existence in the Universe. And all depend upon the advancement of beings in the scale, of which scale the lowest point is the grossest matter, the highest being separated only by the thinnest division from the SPIRIT of THE ALL. And, upward and onward along this Scale of Life, everything is moving. All are on the Path, whose end is THE ALL. All progress is a Returning Home. All is Upward and Onward, in spite of all seemingly contradictory appearances. Such is the message of the Illumined.

The Hermetic Teachings concerning the process of the Mental Creation of the Universe, are that at the beginning of the Creative Cycle, THE ALL, in its aspect of Being, projects its Will toward its aspect of "Becoming" and the process of creation begins. It is taught that the process consists of the lowering of Vibration until a very low degree of vibratory energy is reached, at which point the grossest possible form of Matter is manifested. This process is called the stage of Involution, in which THE ALL becomes "involved," or "wrapped up," in its creation. This process is believed by the Hermetists to have a Correspondence to the mental process of an artist, writer, or inventor, who becomes so wrapped up in his mental creation as to almost forget his own existence and who, for the time being, almost "lives in his creation," If instead of "wrapped" we use the word "rapt," perhaps we will give a better idea of what is meant.

This Involuntary stage of Creation is sometimes called the "Outpouring" of the Divine Energy, just as the Evolutionary state is called the "Indrawing." The extreme pole of the Creative process is considered to be the furthest removed from THE ALL, while the beginning of the Evolutionary stage is regarded as the beginning of the return swing of the pendulum of Rhythm—a "coming home" idea being held in all of the Hermetic Teachings.

The Teachings are that during the "Outpouring," the vibrations become lower and lower until finally the urge ceases, and the return swing begins. But there is this difference, that while in the "Outpouring" the creative forces manifest compactly and as a whole, yet from the beginning of the Evolutionary or "Indrawing" stage, there is manifested the Law of Individualization—that is, the tendency to separate into Units of Force, so that finally that which left THE ALL as unindividualized energy returns to its source as countless highly developed Units of Life, having risen higher and higher in the scale by means of Physical, Mental and Spiritual Evolution.

The ancient Hermetists use the word "Meditation" in describing the process of the mental creation of the Universe in the Mind of THE ALL, the word "Contemplation" also being frequently employed. But the idea intended seems to be that of the employment of the Divine Attention. "Attention" is a word derived from the Latin root, meaning "to reach out; to stretch out," and so the act of Attention is really a mental "reaching out; extension" of mental energy, so that the underlying idea is readily understood when we examine into the real meaning of "Attention."

The Hermetic Teachings regarding the process of Evolution are that, THE ALL, having meditated upon the beginning of the Creation—having thus established the material foundations of the Universe—having thought it into existence—then gradually awakens or rouses from its Meditation and in so doing starts into manifestation the process of Evolution, on the material mental and spiritual planes, successively and in order. Thus the upward movement begins—and all begins to move Spiritward. Matter becomes less gross; the Units spring into being; the combinations begin to form; Life appears and manifests in higher and higher forms; and Mind becomes more and more in evidence—the vibrations constantly becoming higher. In short, the entire process of Evolution, in all of its phases, begins, and proceeds according to the established "Laws of the Indrawing" process. All of this occupies aeons upon aeons of Man's time, each aeon containing countless millions of years, but yet the Illumined inform us that the entire creation, including Involution and Evolution, of an Universe, is but "as the twinkle of the eye" to THE ALL. At the end of countless cycles of aeons of time, THE ALL withdraws its Attention—its Contemplation and Meditation—of the Universe, for the Great Work is finished—and All is withdrawn into THE ALL from which it emerged. But Mystery of Mysteries—the Spirit of each soul is not annihilated, but is infinitely expanded—the Created and the Creator are merged. Such is the report of the Illumined!

The above illustration of the "meditation," and subsequent "awakening from meditation," of THE ALL, is of course but an attempt of the teachers to describe the

Infinite process by a finite example. And, yet: "As Below, so Above." The difference is merely in degree. And just as THE ALL arouses itself from the meditation upon the Universe, so does Man (in time) cease from manifesting upon the Material Plane, and withdraws himself more and more into the Indwelling Spirit, which is indeed "The Divine Ego."

There is one more matter of which we desire to speak in this lesson, and that comes very near to an invasion of the Metaphysical field of speculation, although our purpose is merely to show the futility of such speculation. We allude to the question which inevitably comes to the mind of all thinkers who have ventured to seek the Truth. The question is: "WHY does THE ALL create Universes" The question may be asked in different forms, but the above is the gist of the inquiry.

Men have striven hard to answer this question, but still there is no answer worthy of the name. Some have imagined that THE ALL had something to gain by it, but this is absurd, for what could THE ALL gain that it did not already possess? Others have sought the answer in the idea that THE ALL "wished something to love" and others that it created for pleasure, or amusement; or because it "was lonely" or to manifest its power;—all puerile explanations and ideas, belonging to the childish period of thought.

Others have sought to explain the mystery by assuming that THE ALL found itself "compelled" to create, by reason of its own "internal nature"—its "creative instinct." This idea is in advance of the others, but its weak point lies in the idea of THE ALL being "compelled" by anything, internal or external. If its "internal nature," or "creative instinct," compelled it to do anything, then the "internal nature" or "creative instinct" would be the Absolute, instead of THE ALL, and so accordingly that part of the proposition falls. And, yet, THE ALL does create and manifest, and seems to find some kind of satisfaction in so doing. And it is difficult to escape the conclusion that in some infinite degree it must have what would correspond to an "inner nature," or "creative instinct," in man, with correspondingly infinite Desire and Will. It could not act unless it Willed to Act; and it would not Will to Act, unless it Desired to Act and it would not Desire to Act unless it obtained some Satisfaction thereby. And all of these things would belong to an "Inner Nature," and might be postulated as existing according to the Law of Correspondence. But, still, we prefer to think of THE ALL as acting entirely FREE from any influence, internal as well as external. That is the problem which lies at the root of difficulty—and the difficulty that lies at the root of the problem.

Strictly speaking, there cannot be said to be any "Reason" whatsoever for THE ALL to act, for a "reason" implies a "cause," and THE ALL is above Cause and Effect, except when it Wills to become a Cause, at which time the Principle is set into motion. So, you see, the matter is Unthinkable, just as THE ALL is Unknowable. Just as we say THE ALL merely "IS"—so we are compelled to say that "THE ALL ACTS BECAUSE IT ACTS." At the last, THE ALL is All Reason in Itself; All Law in Itself; All Action in Itself—and it may be said, truthfully, that THE ALL is Its Own Reason; its own Law; its own Act—or still further, that THE ALL; Its Reason; Its Act; is Law; are ONE, all being names for the same thing. In the opinion of those who are giving you these present lessons, the answer is locked up in the INNER SELF of THE ALL, along with its Secret of Being. The Law of Correspondence, in our opinion, reaches only to that aspect of THE ALL, which may be spoken of as "The Aspect of BECOMING." Back of that Aspect is "The Aspect of BEING" in which all Laws are lost in LAW; all Principles merge into PRINCIPLE—and THE ALL; PRINCIPLE; and BEING; are IDENTICAL, ONE AND THE SAME. Therefore, Metaphysical speculation on this point is futile. We go into the matter here, merely to show that we recognize the question, and also the absurdity of the ordinary answers of metaphysics and theology.

In conclusion, it may be of interest to our students to learn that while some of the ancient, and modern, Hermetic Teachers have rather inclined in the direction of applying the Principle of Correspondence to the question, with the result of the "Inner Nature" conclusion,—still the legends have it that HERMES, the Great, when asked this question by his advanced students, answered them by PRESSING HIS LIPS TIGHTLY TOGETHER and saying not a word, indicating that there WAS NO ANSWER. But, then, he may have intended to apply the axiom of his philosophy, that: "The lips of Wisdom are closed, except to the ears of Understanding," believing that even his advanced students did not possess the Understanding which entitled them to the Teaching. At any rate, if Hermes possessed the Secret, he failed to impart it, and so far as the world is concerned THE LIPS OF HERMES ARE CLOSED regarding it. And where the Great Hermes hesitated to speak, what mortal may dare to teach?

But, remember, that whatever be the answer to this problem, if indeed there be an answer the truth remains that: "While All is in THE ALL, it is equally true that THE ALL is in All." The Teaching on this point is emphatic. And, we may add the concluding words of the quotation: "To him who truly understands this truth, hath come great knowledge."

COMMENTARY

The All can be considered an infinite universal mind we are embedded within. We are figments of The All. In the same way that Hamlet is a figment of Shakespeare, so we are a figment of higher intellect or *Nous*. If we follow the symbiotic hierarchy of "as above, so below," Infinite Mind is the source, the universe is mental. That is the foundational principle of *The Kybalion* and Hermeticism itself.

This chapter helps clarify a thorny issue in metaphysics. In modern alternative spirituality we tend to regard it as a truism that "all is one." We criticize something called "duality." I am not sure that framing is helpful. All is connected—all belongs to one substance of mind—but that is not the same as saying "all is one." The tree and the branch are connected but different. The pedal and the stem are connected but different. Here and elsewhere, Atkinson is attempting to impress upon us that we are related to The All but we are not The All. We experience sharply felt limits. These limits may not be ultimate but they are concretely real in the sphere we inhabit. The All is in us but we are not The All.

—MH

Chapter 8

Planes Of Correspondence

"As above, so below; as below, so above."

—THE KYBALION.

The great Second Hermetic Principle embodies the truth that there is a harmony, agreement, and correspondence between the several planes of Manifestation, Life and Being. This truth is a truth because all that is included in the Universe emanates from the same source, and the same laws, principles, and characteristics apply to each unit, or combination of units, of activity, as each manifests its own phenomena upon its own plane.

For the purpose of convenience of thought and study, the Hermetic Philosophy considers that the Universe may be divided into three great classes of phenomena, known as the Three Great Planes, namely:

1. The Great Physical Plane.
2. The Great Mental Plane.
3. The Great Spiritual Plane.

These divisions are more or less artificial and arbitrary, for the truth is that all of the three divisions are but ascending degrees of the great scale of Life, the lowest point of which is undifferentiated Matter, and the highest point that of Spirit. And, moreover, the different Planes shade into each other, so that no hard and fast division may be made between the higher phenomena of the Physical and the lower of the Mental; or between the higher of the Mental and the lower of the Physical.

In short, the Three Great Planes may be regarded as three great groups of degrees of Life Manifestation. While the purposes of this little book do not allow us to enter into an extended discussion of, or explanation of, the subject of these different planes, still we think it well to give a general description of the same at this point.

At the beginning we may as well consider the question so often asked by the neophyte, who desires to be informed regarding the meaning of the word "Plane", which term has been very freely used, and very poorly explained, in many recent works upon the subject of occultism. The question is generally about as follows: "Is a Plane a place having dimensions, or is it merely a condition or state?" We answer: "No, not a place, nor ordinary dimension of space; and yet more than a state or condition. It may be considered as a state or condition, and yet the state or condition is a degree of dimension, in a scale subject to measurement." Somewhat paradoxical, is it not? But let us examine the matter. A "dimension," you know, is "a measure in a straight line, relating to measure," etc. The ordinary dimensions of space are length, breadth, and height, or perhaps length, breadth, height, thickness or circumference. But there is another dimension of "created things" or "measure in a straight line," known to occultists, and to scientists as well, although the latter have not as yet applied the term "dimension" to it—and this new dimension, which, by the way, is the much speculated-about "Fourth Dimension," is the standard used in determining the degrees or "planes."

This Fourth Dimension may be called "The Dimension of Vibration" It is a fact well known to modern science, as well as to the Hermetists who have embodied the truth in their "Third Hermetic Principle," that "everything is in motion; everything vibrates; nothing is at rest." From the highest manifestation, to the lowest, everything and all things Vibrate. Not only do they vibrate at different rates of motion, but as in different directions and in a different manner. The degrees of the rate of vibrations constitute the degrees of measurement on the Scale of Vibrations—in other words the degrees of the Fourth Dimension. And these degrees form what occultists call "Planes" The higher the degree of rate of vibration, the higher the plane, and the higher the manifestation of Life occupying that plane. So that while a plane is not "a place," nor yet "a state or condition," yet it possesses qualities common to both. We shall have more to say regarding the subject of the scale of Vibrations in our next lessons, in which we shall consider the Hermetic Principle of Vibration.

You will kindly remember, however, that the Three Great Planes are not actual divisions of the phenomena of the Universe, but merely arbitrary terms used by the Hermetists in order to aid in the thought and study of the various degrees and Forms of universal activity and life. The atom of matter, the unit of force, the mind of man, and the being of the arch-angel are all but degrees in one scale, and all fundamentally the same, the difference between solely a matter of degree, and rate of vibration— all are creations of THE ALL, and have their existence solely within the Infinite Mind of THE ALL.

The Hermetists sub-divide each of the Three Great Planes into Seven Minor Planes, and each of these latter are also sub-divided into seven sub-planes, all divisions being more or less arbitrary, shading into each other, and adopted merely for convenience of scientific study and thought.

The Great Physical Plane, and its Seven Minor Planes, is that division of the phenomena of the Universe which includes all that relates to physics, or material things, forces, and manifestations. It includes all forms of that which we call Matter, and all forms of that which we call Energy or Force. But you must remember that the Hermetic Philosophy does not recognize Matter as a thing in itself, or as having a separate existence even in the Mind of THE ALL. The Teachings are that Matter is but a form of Energy—that is, Energy at a low rate of vibrations of a certain kind. And accordingly the Hermetists classify Matter under the head of Energy, and give to it three of the Seven Minor Planes of the Great Physical Plane.

These Seven Minor Physical Planes are as follows:

1. The Plane of Matter (A)
2. The Plane of Matter (B)
3. The Plane of Matter (C)
4. The Plane of Ethereal Substance
5. The Plane of Energy (A)
6. The Plane of Energy (B)
7. The Plane of Energy (C)

The Plane of Matter (A) comprises the forms of Matter in its form of solids, liquids, and gases, as generally recognized by the text-books on physics. The Plane of Matter (B) comprises certain higher and more subtle forms of Matter of the existence of which modern science is but now recognizing, the phenomena of Radiant Matter, in its phases of radium, etc., belonging to the lower subdivision of this Minor Plane. The Plane of Matter (C) comprises forms of the most subtle and tenuous Matter, the existence of which is not suspected by ordinary scientists. The Plane of Ethereal Substance comprises that which science speaks of as "The Ether," a substance of extreme tenuity and elasticity, pervading all Universal Space, and acting as a medium for the transmission of waves of energy, such as light, heat, electricity, etc. This Ethereal Substance forms a connecting link between Matter (so-called) and Energy, and partakes of the nature of each. The Hermetic Teachings, however, instruct that this plane has seven sub-divisions (as have all of the Minor Planes), and that in fact there are seven ethers, instead of but one.

Next above the Plane of Ethereal Substance comes the Plane of Energy (A), which comprises the ordinary forms of Energy known to science, its seven sub-planes being, respectively, Heat; Light; Magnetism; Electricity, and Attraction (including Gravitation, Cohesion, Chemical Affinity, etc.) and several other forms of energy indicated by scientific experiments but not as yet named or classified. The Plane of Energy (B) comprises seven subplanes of higher forms of energy not as yet discovered by science, but which have been called "Nature's Finer Forces" and which are called into operation in manifestations of certain forms of mental phenomena, and by which such phenomena becomes possible. The Plane of Energy (C) comprises seven sub-planes of energy so highly organized that it bears many of the characteristics of "life," but which is not recognized by the minds of men on the ordinary plane of development, being available for the use on beings of the Spiritual Plane alone—such energy is unthinkable to ordinary man, and may be considered almost as "the divine power." The beings employing the same are as "gods" compared even to the highest human types known to us.

The Great Mental Plane comprises those forms of "living things" known to us in ordinary life, as well as certain other forms not so well known except to the occultist. The classification of the Seven Minor Mental Planes is more or less satisfactory and arbitrary (unless accompanied by elaborate explanations which are foreign to the purpose of this particular work), but we may as well mention them. They are as follows:

1. The Plane of Mineral Mind
2. The Plane of Elemental Mind (A)
3. The Plane of Plant Mind
4. The Plane of Elemental Mind (B)
5. The Plane of Animal Mind
6. The Plane of Elemental Mind (C)
7. The Plane of Human Mind

The Plane of Mineral Mind comprises the "states or conditions" of the units or entities, or groups and combinations of the same, which animate the forms known to us as "minerals, chemicals, etc." These entities must not be confounded with the molecules, atoms and corpuscles themselves, the latter being merely the material bodies or forms of these entities, just as a man's body is but his material form and not "himself." These entities may be called "souls" in one sense, and are living beings of a low degree of development, life, and mind—just a little more than the units of "living energy" which comprise the higher subdivisions of the highest Physical Plane. The average mind does not generally attribute the possession of mind, soul, or life, to the mineral kingdom, but all occultists recognize the existence of the same, and modern science is rapidly moving forward to the point-of-view of the Hermetic, in this respect. The molecules, atoms and corpuscles have their "loves and hates"; "likes and dislikes"; "attractions and repulsions"; "affinities and non-affinities," etc., and some of the more daring of modern scientific minds have expressed the opinion that the desire and will, emotions and feelings, of the atoms differ only in degree from those of men. We have no time or space to argue this matter here. All occultists know it to be a fact, and others are referred to some of the more recent scientific works for outside corroboration. There are the usual seven subdivisions to this plane.

The Plane of Elemental Mind (A) comprises the state or condition, and degree of mental and vital development of a class of entities unknown to the average man, but recognized to occultists. They are invisible to the ordinary senses of man, but, nevertheless, exist and play their part of the Drama of the Universe. Their degree of intelligence is between that of the mineral and chemical entities on the one hand, and of the entities of the plant kingdom on the other. There are seven subdivisions to this plane, also.

The Plane of Plant Mind, in its seven sub-divisions, comprises the states or conditions of the entities comprising the kingdoms of the Plant World, the vital and mental phenomena of which is fairly well understood by the average intelligent person, many new and interesting scientific works regarding "Mind and Life in Plants" having been published during the last decade. Plants have life, mind and "souls," as well as have the animals, man, and super-man.

The Plane of Elemental Mind (B), in its seven sub-divisions, comprises the states and conditions of a higher form of "elemental" or unseen entities, playing their part in the general work of the Universe, the mind and life of which form a part of the scale between the Plane of Plant Mind and the Plane of Animal Mind, the entities partaking of the nature of both.

The Plane of Animal Mind, in its seven sub-divisions, comprises the states and conditions of the entities, beings, or souls, animating the animal forms of life, familiar to us all. It is not necessary to go into details regarding this kingdom or plane of life, for the animal world is as familiar to us as is our own.

The Plane of Elemental Mind (C), in its seven sub-divisions, comprises those entities or beings, invisible as are all such elemental forms, which partake of the nature of both animal and human life in a degree and in certain combinations. The highest forms are semi-human in intelligence.

The Plane of Human Mind, in its seven sub-divisions, comprises those manifestations of life and mentality which are common to Man, in his various grades, degrees, and divisions. In this connection, we wish to point out the fact that the average man of today occupies but the fourth sub-division of the Plane of Human Mind, and only the most intelligent have crossed the borders of the Fifth Sub-Division. It has taken the race millions of years to reach this stage, and it will take many more years for the race to move on to the sixth and seventh sub-divisions, and beyond. But, remember, that there have been races before us which have passed through these degrees, and then on to higher planes. Our own race is the fifth (with stragglers from the fourth) which has set foot upon The Path. And, then there are a few advanced souls of our own race who have outstripped the masses, and who have passed on to the sixth and seventh sub-division, and some few being still further on. The man of the Sixth Sub-Division will be "The Super-Man"; he of the Seventh will be "The Over-Man."

In our consideration of the Seven Minor Mental Planes, we have merely referred to the Three Elementary Planes in a general way. We do not wish to go into this subject in detail in this work, for it does not belong to this part of the general philosophy and teachings. But we may say this much, in order to give you a little clearer idea, of the relations of these planes to the more familiar ones—the Elementary Planes bear the same relation to the Planes of Mineral, Plant, Animal and Human Mentality and Life, that the black keys on the piano do to the white keys. The white keys are sufficient to produce music, but there are certain scales, melodies, and harmonies, in which the black keys play their part, and in which their presence is necessary. They are also necessary as "connecting links" of soul-condition; entity states, etc., between the several other planes, certain forms of development being attained therein—this last fact giving to the reader who can "read between the lines" a new light upon the processes of Evolution, and a new key to the secret door of the "leaps of life" between kingdom and kingdom. The great kingdoms of Elementals are fully recognized by all occultists, and the esoteric writings are full of mention of them. The readers of Bulwer's "Sanoni" and similar tales will recognize the entities inhabiting these planes of life.

Passing on from the Great Mental Plane to the Great Spiritual Plane, what shall we say? How can we explain these higher states of Being, Life and Mind, to minds as yet unable to grasp and understand the higher subdivisions of the Plane of Human Mind? The task is impossible. We can speak only in the most general terms. How may Light be described to a man born blind—how sugar, to a man who has never tasted anything sweet—how harmony, to one born deaf?

All that we can say is that the Seven Minor Planes of the Great Spiritual Plane (each Minor Plane having its seven sub-divisions) comprise Beings possessing Life, Mind and Form as far above that of Man of to-day as the latter is above the earth-worm, mineral or even certain forms of Energy or Matter. The Life of these Beings so far transcends ours, that we cannot even think of the details of the same; their minds so far transcend ours, that to them we scarcely seem to "think," and our mental processes seem almost akin to material processes; the Matter of which their forms are composed is of the highest Planes of Matter, nay, some are even said to be "clothed in Pure Energy." What may be said of such Beings?

On the Seven Minor Planes of the Great Spiritual Plane exist Beings of whom we may speak as Angels; Archangels; Demi-Gods. On the lower Minor Planes dwell those great souls whom we call Masters and Adepts. Above them come the Great Hierarchies of the Angelic Hosts, unthinkable to man; and above those come those who may without irreverence be called "The Gods," so high in the scale of Being are they, their being, intelligence and power being akin to those attributed by the races of men to their conceptions of Deity. These Beings are beyond even the highest flights of the human imagination, the word "Divine" being the only one applicable to them. Many of these Beings, as well as the Angelic Host, take the greatest interest in the affairs of the Universe and play an important part in its affairs. These Unseen Divinities and Angelic Helpers extend their influence freely and powerfully, in the process of Evolution, and Cosmic Progress. Their occasional intervention and assistance in human affairs have led to the many legends, beliefs, religions and traditions of the race, past and present. They have super-imposed their knowledge and power upon the world, again and again, all under the Law of THE ALL, of course.

But, yet, even the highest of these advanced Beings exist merely as creations of, and in, the Mind of THE ALL, and are subject to the Cosmic Processes and Universal Laws. They are still Mortal. We may call them "gods" if we like, but still they are but the Elder Brethren of the Race,—the advanced souls who have outstripped their brethren, and who have foregone the ecstasy of Absorption by THE ALL, in order to help the race on its upward journey along The Path. But, they belong to the Universe, and are subject to its conditions—they are mortal—and their plane is below that of Absolute Spirit.

Only the most advanced Hermetists are able to grasp the Inner Teachings regarding the state of existence, and the powers manifested on the Spiritual Planes. The phenomena is so much higher than that of the Mental Planes that a confusion of ideas would surely result from an attempt to describe the same. Only those whose minds have been carefully trained along the lines of the Hermetic Philosophy for years—yes, those who have brought with them from other incarnations the knowledge acquired previously—can comprehend just what is meant by the Teaching regarding these Spiritual Planes. And much of these Inner Teachings is held by the Hermetists as being too sacred, important and even dangerous for general public dissemination. The intelligent student may recognize what we mean by this when we state that the meaning of "Spirit" as used by the Hermetists is akin to "Living Power"; "Animated Force;" "Inner Essence;" "Essence of Life," etc., which meaning must not be confounded with that usually and commonly employed in connection with the term, i.e., "religious; ecclesiastical; spiritual; ethereal; holy," etc., etc. To occultists the word "Spirit" is used in the sense of "The Animating Principle," carrying with it the idea of Power, Living Energy, Mystic Force, etc. And occultists know that that which is known to them as "Spiritual Power" may be employed for evil as well as good ends (in accordance with the Principle of Polarity), a fact which has been recognized by the majority of religions in their conceptions of Satan, Beelzebub, the Devil, Lucifer, Fallen Angels, etc. And so the knowledge regarding these Planes has been kept in the Holy of Holies in all Esoteric Fraternities and Occult Orders, in the Secret Chamber of the Temple. But this may be said here, that those who have attained high spiritual powers and have misused them, have a terrible fate in store for them, and the swing of the pendulum of Rhythm will inevitably swing them back to the furthest extreme of Material existence, from which point they must retrace their steps Spiritward, along the weary rounds of The Path, but always with the added torture of having always with them a lingering memory of the heights from which they fell owing to their evil actions. The legends of the Fallen Angels have a basis in actual facts, as all advanced occultists know. The striving for selfish power on the Spiritual Planes inevitably results in the selfish soul losing its spiritual balance and falling back as far as it had previously risen. But to even such a soul, the opportunity of a return is given—and such souls make the return journey, paying the terrible penalty according to the invariable Law.

In conclusion we would again remind you that according to the Principle of Correspondence, which embodies the truth: "As Above so Below; as Below, so Above," all of the Seven Hermetic Principles are in full operation on all of the many planes, Physical Mental and Spiritual. The Principle of Mental Substance of course applies to all the planes, for all are held in the Mind of THE ALL. The Principle of Correspondence manifests in all, for there is a correspondence, harmony and agreement between the several planes. The Principle of Vibration manifests on all planes, in fact the very differences that go to make the "planes" arise from Vibration, as we have explained. The Principle of Polarity manifests on each plane, the extremes of the Poles being apparently opposite and contradictory. The Principle of Rhythm manifests on each Plane, the movement of the phenomena having its ebb and flow, rise and flow, incoming and outgoing. The Principle of Cause and Effect manifests on each Plane, every Effect having its Cause and every Cause having its effect. The Principle of Gender manifests on each Plane, the Creative Energy being always manifest, and operating along the lines of its Masculine and Feminine Aspects.

"As Above so Below; as Below, so Above." This centuries old Hermetic axiom embodies one of the great Principles of Universal Phenomena. As we proceed with our consideration of the remaining Principles, we will see even more clearly the truth of the universal nature of this great Principle of Correspondence.

COMMENTARY

Many readers find this chapter difficult because of its extensive cosmology. I find some of that material fore-sightful because it suggests a correspondence to string theory, which I consider in the next commentary. But for our purposes here, I want to focus on the second Hermetic principle highlighted in this chapter, the *law of correspondence*.

The law of correspondence is really another sounding of "as above, so below." All is interrelated. Everything you experience is intimately linked to and reflective of the nature of the whole. It is impossible to talk about any unit of life, any experience, or any phe-nomena as unattached to and unaffected by the symbi-otic universe that surrounds it. Change one thing and you change everything.

Hence, one change in your conduct could produce extraordinary and unforeseeable ripple effects.

Philosopher William James (1842–1910) made refer-ence to this phenomenon. James noted that if you exer-cise one act of self-determination, whether it means starting a cherished project, resisting a bad habit, or desisting from an act of gossip you have no idea of the network of possibility that you may be tapping into. Everything relates. In 1907, James wrote in his essay "The Energies of Men:"

It is notorious that a single successful effort of moral volition, such as saying "no" to some habitual temptation, or performing some courageous act, will launch a man on a higher level of energy for days and weeks, will give him a new range of power.

Years ago a spiritual teacher whom I deeply admired encouraged me to write a conciliatory letter to my father from whom I was estranged. My father and I had a rupture when I was eighteen. The teacher told me, in effect, if you write this letter to your father, you have no idea what kinds of possibilities it might fertilize. You have a chain of ancestry that may be positively affected. Perhaps such a letter will work its way through your entire network ancestors, solving a problem, healing a rupture. Gurdjieff observed that the past controls the future, but the present controls the past.

I took his advice and wrote that letter. I never heard back. I do not know whether it fertilized other possibilities, or whether it even arrived. But I have always looked back on that moment as one where I did the best of which I'm capable, and I accepted the possibility that change is symbiotic. Having sent this letter, I also know that this situation is not something I'll have to look back as unfinished business at the end of the road. My hope is that the letter did something positive, something I may never see, for its recipient or others.

This story illustrates something about the second Hermetic principle of correspondences. Since everything is related, we never know and never can fully know, how an act will reverberate. Rather than shrinking from this, allow it to give you a sense of power. Just imagine: if you refuse to listen to or spread a piece of gossip about someone you could be saving a life. I mean that in the plainest sense. People have no idea the power they possess. That's inherent in Hermetic law.

—MH

Chapter 9

Vibration

"Nothing rests; everything moves; everything vibrates."
—THE KYBALION.

The great Third Hermetic Principle—the Principle of Vibration—embodies the truth that Motion is manifest in everything in the Universe—that nothing is at rest—that everything moves, vibrates, and circles. This Hermetic Principle was recognized by some of the early Greek philosophers who embodied it in their systems. But, then, for centuries it was lost sight of by the thinkers outside of the Hermetic ranks. But in the Nineteenth Century physical science re-discovered the truth and the Twentieth Century scientific discoveries have added additional proof of the correctness and truth of this centuries-old Hermetic doctrine.

The Hermetic Teachings are that not only is everything in constant movement and vibration, but that the "differences" between the various manifestations of the universal power are due entirely to the varying rate and mode of vibrations. Not only this, but that even THE ALL, in itself, manifests a constant vibration of such an infinite degree of intensity and rapid motion that it may be practically considered as at rest, the teachers directing the attention of the students to the fact that even on the physical plane a rapidly moving object (such as a revolving wheel) seems to be at rest. The Teachings are to the effect that Spirit is at one end of the Pole of Vibration, the other Pole being certain extremely gross forms of Matter. Between these two poles are millions upon millions of different rates and modes of vibration.

Modern Science has proven that all that we call Matter and Energy are but "modes of vibratory motion," and some of the more advanced scientists are rapidly moving toward the positions of the occultists who hold that the phenomena of Mind are likewise modes of vibration or motion. Let us see what science has to say regarding the question of vibrations in matter and energy.

In the first place, science teaches that all matter manifests, in some degree, the vibrations arising from temperature or heat. Be an object cold or hot—both being but degrees of the same things—it manifests certain heat vibrations, and in that sense is in motion and vibration. Then all particles of Matter are in circular movement, from corpuscle to suns. The planets revolve around suns, and many of them turn on their axes. The suns move around greater central points, and these are believed to move around still greater, and so on, ad infinitum. The molecules of which the particular kinds of Matter are composed are in a state of constant vibration and movement around each other and against each other. The molecules are composed of Atoms, which, likewise, are in a state of constant movement and vibration. The atoms are composed of Corpuscles, sometimes called "electrons," "ions," etc., which also are in a state of rapid motion, revolving around each other, and which manifest a very rapid state and mode of vibration. And, so we see that all forms of Matter manifest Vibration, in accordance with the Hermetic Principle of Vibration.

And so it is with the various forms of Energy. Science teaches that Light, Heat, Magnetism and Electricity are but forms of vibratory motion connected in some way with, and probably emanating from the Ether. Science does not as yet attempt to explain the nature of the phenomena known as Cohesion, which is the principle of Molecular Attraction; nor Chemical Affinity, which is the principle of Atomic Attraction; nor Gravitation (the greatest mystery of the three), which is the principle of attraction by which every particle or mass of Matter is bound to every other particle or mass. These three forms of Energy are not as yet understood by science, yet the writers incline to the opinion that these too are manifestations of some form of vibratory energy, a fact which the Hermetists have held and taught for ages past.

The Universal Ether, which is postulated by science without its nature being understood clearly, is held by the Hermetists to be but a higher manifestation of that which is erroneously called matter—that is to say, Matter at a higher degree of vibration—and is called by them "The Ethereal Substance." The Hermetists teach that this Ethereal Substance is of extreme tenuity and elasticity, and pervades universal space, serving as a medium of transmission of waves of vibratory energy, such as heat, light, electricity, magnetism, etc. The Teachings are that The Ethereal Substance is a connecting link between the forms of vibratory energy known as "Matter" on the one hand, and "Energy or Force" on the other; and also that it manifests a degree of vibration, in rate and mode, entirely its own.

Scientists have offered the illustration of a rapidly moving wheel, top, or cylinder, to show the effects of increasing rates of vibration. The illustration supposes a wheel, top, or revolving cylinder, running at a low rate of speed—we will call this revolving thing "the object" in following out the illustration. Let us suppose the object moving slowly. It may be seen readily, but no sound of its movement reaches the ear. The speed is gradually increased. In a few moments its movement becomes so rapid that a deep growl or low note may be heard. Then as the rate is increased the note rises one in the musical scale. Then, the motion being still further increased, the next highest note is distinguished. Then, one after another, all the notes of the musical scale appear, rising higher and higher as the motion is increased. Finally when the motions have reached a certain rate the final note perceptible to human ears is reached and the shrill, piercing shriek dies away, and silence follows. No sound is heard from the revolving object, the rate of motion being so high that the human ear cannot register the vibrations. Then comes the perception of rising degrees of Heat. Then after quite a time the eye catches a glimpse of the object becoming a dull dark reddish color. As the rate increases, the red becomes brighter. Then as the speed is increased, the red melts into an orange. Then the orange melts into a yellow. Then follow, successively, the shades of green, blue, indigo, and finally violet, as the rate of sped increases. Then the violet shades away, and all color disappears, the human eye not being able to register them. But there are invisible rays emanating from the revolving object, the rays that are used in photographing, and other subtle rays of light. Then begin to manifest the peculiar rays known as the "X Rays," etc., as the constitution of the object changes. Electricity and Magnetism are emitted when the appropriate rate of vibration is attained.

When the object reaches a certain rate of vibration its molecules disintegrate, and resolve themselves into the original elements or atoms. Then the atoms, following the Principle of Vibration, are separated into the countless corpuscles of which they are composed. And finally, even the corpuscles disappear and the object may be said to Be composed of The Ethereal Substance. Science does not dare to follow the illustration further, but the Hermetists teach that if the vibrations be continually increased the object would mount up the successive states of manifestation and would in turn manifest the various mental stages, and then on Spiritward, until it would finally re-enter THE ALL, which is Absolute Spirit. The "object," however, would have ceased to be an "object" long before the stage of Ethereal Substance was reached, but otherwise the illustration is correct inasmuch as it shows the effect of constantly increased rates and modes of vibration. It must be remembered, in the above illustration, that at the stages at which the "object" throws off vibrations of light, heat, etc., it is not actually "resolved" into those forms of energy (which are much higher in the scale), but simply that it reaches a degree of vibration in which those forms of energy are liberated, in a degree, from the confining influences of its molecules, atoms and corpuscles, as the case may be. These forms of energy, although much higher in the scale than matter, are imprisoned and confined in the material combinations, by reason of the energies manifesting through, and using material forms, but thus becoming entangled and confined in their creations of material forms, which, to an extent, is true of all creations, the creating force becoming involved in its creation.

But the Hermetic Teachings go much further than do those of modern science. They teach that all manifestation of thought, emotion, reason, will or desire, or any mental state or condition, are accompanied by vibrations, a portion of which are thrown off and which tend to affect the minds of other persons by "induction." This is the principle which produces the phenomena of "telepathy"; mental influence, and other forms of the action and power of mind over mind, with which the general public is rapidly becoming acquainted, owing to the wide dissemination of occult knowledge by the various schools, cults and teachers along these lines at this time.

Every thought, emotion or mental state has its corresponding rate and mode of vibration. And by an effort of the will of the person, or of other persons, these mental states may be reproduced, just as a musical tone may be reproduced by causing an instrument to vibrate at a certain rate—just as color may be reproduced in the same may. By a knowledge of the Principle of Vibration, as applied to Mental Phenomena, one may polarize his mind at any degree he wishes, thus gaining a perfect control over his mental states, moods, etc. In the same way he may affect the minds of others, producing the desired mental states in them. In short, he may be able to produce on the Mental Plane that which science produces on the Physical Plane—namely, "Vibrations at Will." This power of course may be acquired only by the proper instruction, exercises, practice, etc., the science being that of Mental Transmutation, one of the branches of the Hermetic Art.

A little reflection on what we have said will show the student that the Principle of Vibration underlies the wonderful phenomena of the power manifested by the Masters and Adepts, who are able to apparently set aside the Laws of Nature, but who, in reality, are simply using one law against another; one principle against others; and who accomplish their results by changing the vibrations of material objects, or forms of energy, and thus perform what are commonly called "miracles."

As one of the old Hermetic writers has truly said: "He who understands the Principle of Vibration, has grasped the scepter of Power."

COMMENTARY

The third principle of *The Kybalion* is *all is in vibration*. It's an interesting observation because this book was, of course, written in 1908 and drew upon ideas that were themselves ancient. If you speak with a quantum physicist today he or she would probably agree that everything is in vibration to the extent that we understand subatomic particles occupy a state of infinitude or superposition. They appear everywhere at once and localize at a fixed point only when an observer takes a measurement. A law of universal movement prevails on the subatomic scale.

Another facet of this principle relates to string theory. String theorists attempt to explain the strange behavior of subatomic objects, including why such objects affect one another at distances, and why, as Newton observed, even macro objects at vast removes mirror each other's motions. String theory holds that all particles and all matter are not separate entities but rather are part of vast, undulating networks of strings. When an object at one point in space affects another object, we're not seeing two distinct entities but a unified string of objects. What's more, different dimensions and universes exist along these strings, so we may not always see the thing that is causing an effect. In string theory, all material and events are all one. We catch only hints of this through exquisitely fine measurement.

The Kybalion employs the concept of vibration to suggest that all of life is permeable and in constant motion. Hence, if all is mental, if all corresponds, and if there exists constant permeability, then it stands to reason that nothing is fixed, whether psychologically, relationally, circumstantially, or physically. Matter is not fixed. There is constant and lawful change. The principles of mutability, transformation, and metamorphosis are ever at work.

The term vibration is sometimes considered a spiritual trope. The author's use of the term could be defended in terms of the hard sciences, but it's not necessary to defend. You could think of it as a metaphor. If you prefer, use the term mutability. That's the principle Atkinson is driving at. All is in vibration, all is changing, all is dynamic. The finer the matter, the higher the rate of vibration. This may be why subatomic particles are everywhere at once, or in a wave state. They localize only upon observation. Mind, the finest of instruments, is the prime factor in this phenomenon.   —MH

Chapter 10

Polarity

"Everything is dual; everything has poles; everything has its pair of opposites; like and unlike are the same; opposites are identical in nature, but different in degree; extremes meet; all truths are but half-truths; all paradoxes may be reconciled."
—THE KYBALION.

The great Fourth Hermetic Principle—the Principle of Polarity embodies the truth that all manifested things have "two sides"; "two aspects"; "two poles"; a "pair of opposites," with manifold degrees between the two extremes. The old paradoxes, which have ever perplexed the mind of men, are explained by an understanding of this Principle. Man has always recognized something akin to this Principle, and has endeavored to express it by such sayings, maxims and aphorisms as the following: "Everything is and isn't, at the same time"; "all truths are but half-truths"; "every truth is half-false"; "there are two sides to everything"; "there is a reverse side to every shield," etc., etc.

The Hermetic Teachings are to the effect that the difference between things seemingly diametrically opposed to each other is merely a matter of degree. It teaches that "the pairs of opposites may be reconciled," and that "thesis and anti-thesis are identical in nature, but different in degree"; and that the "universal reconciliation of opposites" is effected by a recognition of this Principle of Polarity. The teachers claim that illustrations of this Principle may be had on every hand, and from an examination into the real nature of anything. They begin by showing that Spirit and Matter are but the two poles of the same thing, the intermediate planes being merely degrees of vibration. They show that THE ALL and The Many are the same, the difference being merely a matter of degree of Mental Manifestation. Thus the LAW and Laws are the two opposite poles of one thing. Likewise, PRINCIPLE and Principles. Infinite Mind and finite minds.

Then passing on to the Physical Plane, they illustrate the Principle by showing that Heat and Cold are identical in nature, the differences being merely a matter of degrees. The thermometer shows many degrees of temperature, the lowest pole being called "cold," and the highest "heat." Between these two poles are many degrees of "heat" or "cold," call them either and you are equally correct. The higher of two degrees is always "warmer," while the lower is always "colder." There is no absolute standard—all is a matter of degree. There is no place on the thermometer where heat ceases and cold begins. It is all a matter of higher or lower vibrations. The very terms "high" and "low," which we are compelled to use, are but poles of the same thing—the terms are relative. So with "East and West"—travel around the world in an eastward direction, and you reach a point which is called west at your starting point, and you return from that westward point. Travel far enough North, and you will find yourself traveling South, or vice versa.

Light and Darkness are poles of the same thing, with many degrees between them. The musical scale is the same—starting with "C" you move upward until you reach another "C" and so on, the differences between the two ends of the board being the same, with many degrees between the two extremes. The scale of color is the same—higher and lower vibrations being the only difference between high violet and low red. Large and Small are relative. So are Noise and Quiet; Hard and Soft follow the rule. Likewise Sharp and Dull. Positive and Negative are two poles of the same thing, with countless degrees between them.

Good and Bad are not absolute—we call one end of the scale Good and the other Bad, or one end Good and the other Evil, according to the use of the terms. A thing is "less good" than the thing higher in the scale; but that "less good" thing, in turn, is "more good" than the thing next below it—and so on, the "more or less" being regulated by the position on the scale.

And so it is on the Mental Plane. "Love and Hate" are generally regarded as being things diametrically opposed to each other; entirely different; unreconcilable. But we apply the Principle of Polarity; we find that there is no such thing as Absolute Love or Absolute Hate, as distinguished from each other. The two are merely terms applied to the two poles of the same thing. Beginning at any point of the scale we find "more love," or "less hate," as we ascend the scale; and "more hate" or "less love" as we descend this being true no matter from what point, high or low, we may start. There are degrees of Love and Hate, and there is a middle point where "Like and Dislike" become so faint that it is difficult to distinguish between them. Courage and Fear come under the same rule. The Pairs of Opposites exist everywhere. Where you find one thing you find its opposite—the two poles.

And it is this fact that enables the Hermetist to transmute one mental state into another, along the lines of Polarization. Things belonging to different classes cannot be transmuted into each other, but things of the same class may be changed, that is, may have their polarity changed. Thus Love never becomes East or West, or Red or Violet—but it may and often does turn into Hate—and likewise Hate may be transformed into Love, by changing its polarity. Courage may be transmuted into Fear, and the reverse. Hard things may be rendered Soft. Dull things become Sharp. Hot things become Cold. And so on, the transmutation always being between things of the same kind of different degrees. Take the case of a Fearful man. By raising his mental vibrations along the line of Fear-Courage, he can be filled with the highest degree of Courage and Fearlessness. And, likewise, the Slothful man may change himself into an Active, Energetic individual simply by polarizing along the lines of the desired quality.

The student who is familiar with the processes by which the various schools of Mental Science, etc., produce changes in the mental states of those following their teachings, may not readily understand the principle underlying many of these changes. When, however, the Principle of Polarity is once grasped, and it is seen that the mental changes are occasioned by a change of polarity—a sliding along the same scale—the hatter is readily understood. The change is not in the nature of a transmutation of one thing into another thing entirely different—but is merely a change of degree in the same things, a vastly important difference. For instance, borrowing an analogy from the Physical Plane, it is impossible to change Heat into Sharpness, Loudness, Highness, etc., but Heat may readily be transmuted into Cold, simply by lowering the vibrations. In the same way Hate and Love are mutually transmutable; so are Fear and Courage. But Fear cannot be transformed into Love, nor can Courage be transmuted into Hate. The mental states belong to innumerable classes, each class of which has its opposite poles, along which transmutation is possible.

The student will readily recognize that in the mental states, as well as in the phenomena of the Physical Plane, the two poles may be classified as Positive and Negative, respectively. Thus Love is Positive to Hate; Courage to Fear; Activity to Non-Activity, etc., etc. And it will also be noticed that even to those unfamiliar with the Principle of Vibration, the Positive pole seems to be of a higher degree than the Negative, and readily dominates it. The tendency of Nature is in the direction of the dominant activity of the Positive pole.

In addition to the changing of the poles of one's own mental states by the operation of the art of Polarization, the phenomena of Mental Influence, in its manifold phases, shows us that the principle may be extended so as to embrace the phenomena of the influence of one mind over that of another, of which so much has been written and taught of late years. When it is understood that Mental Induction is possible, that is that mental states may be produced by "induction" from others, then we can readily see how a certain rate of vibration, or polarization of a certain mental state, may be communicated to another person, and his polarity in that class of mental states thus changed. It is along this principle that the results of many of the "mental treatments" are obtained. For instance, a person is "blue," melancholy and full of fear. A mental scientist bringing his own mind up to the desired vibration by his trained will, and thus obtaining the desired polarization in his own case, then produces a similar mental state in the other by induction, the result being that the vibrations are raised and the person polarizes toward the Positive end of the scale instead toward the Negative, and his Fear and other negative emotions are transmuted to Courage and similar positive mental states. A little study will show you that these mental changes are nearly all along the line of Polarization, the change being one of degree rather than of kind.

A knowledge of the existence of this great Hermetic Principle will enable the student to better understand his own mental states, and those of other people. He will see that these states are all matters of degree, and seeing thus, he will be able to raise or lower the vibration at will—to change his mental poles, and thus be Master of his mental states, instead of being their servant and slave. And by his knowledge he will be able to aid his fellows intelligently and by the appropriate methods change the polarity when the same is desirable. We advise all students to familiarize themselves with this Principle of Polarity, for a correct understanding of the same will throw light on many difficult subjects.

COMMENTARY

The fourth Hermetic principle is *the law of polarity*. This may be the most practical idea in *The Kybalion*. I see almost everything in the book as a preface and epilogue to the principle of polarity.

The concept is simple: everything in life belongs to a sliding scale and balances between two polarities. This is true physically, in terms of hot and cold, and it is also true emotionally. Every emotion that you experience is simply a point on a scale relating to an equal and opposite point. For example, fear and courage are part of a sliding scale. Love and hate are part of a sliding scale. Enthusiasm and boredom are part of a sliding scale. Depression and exuberance are part of a sliding scale. Life rarely exists at the extreme ends of these polarities but is often balanced in between.

According to the law of polarity, you possess the ability to *shift* an emotional experience to its opposing point. To enact this shift you direct your attention to the opposite quality. For example, let's say that you're fearful. And you understand that fear is the opposing polarity of courage. If you use every intellectual and emotional resource available to you, and you concentrate *not on eradicating fear* but on cultivating courage, you will experience a sliding of the scale, a swinging of the pendulum, from cowardice to courage. That's the contention of the principle of polarity. The key is functioning along the sliding scale.

You see this occur all the time. People have feelings of love or infatuation for someone, and then they hate or disdain this person. When someone is found murdered, who's the first suspect? Passions function along a sliding scale. The act of purposefully reversing polarity requires effort. Do not be discouraged if you try and fail. Certain attitudes and emotion reactions have been cemented into you through years of conditioning. You have temperamental proclivities. It shouldn't be easy. But it is a fact that everything has its polar opposite and hence everything can be changed, at times quickly.

If you fail it may be because you have not accurately identified the opposing polarity. We are not always aware of the opposing polarity within ourselves. In a 1988 speech at Georgetown University, I heard ethicist Elie Wiesel say that the opposite of love is not hate but indifference. For years I considered that a profound insight. But, whatever its merits, I came to see it as untrue—because in matters of passion I believe that the love-hate continuum is clearer, plainer, and more specifically attached to the sexual energies. Indifference is probably the opposite of empathy. One of the most confounding questions of emotional polarity involves anger. What is the opposite of anger? For me, it is power. Anger is an expression of helplessness. True power is calm command and natural ease. It matters less what you call something than accurately identifying the *feeling* involved. This requires inner experiment. You are an emotional alchemist.

I mentioned that the principle of polarity applies physically: hot and cold, parched and aquafied, gaseous and solid. Depending upon changes in conditions, all things will slide to their opposite—but to be an opposite, it must be of the *same kind*. You cannot change one thing into another that is outside of its nature. The ancient alchemists sought, both literally and metaphorically, to change base metal into gold. That is a continuum. But you cannot change an emotion, such as sorrow, into matter, such as marble. The change must occur within the same category.   —MH

Chapter 11

Rhythm

*"Everything flows out and in; everything has its
tides; all things rise and fall; the pendulum-swing
manifests in everything; the measure of the swing
to the right, is the measure of the swing to the left;
rhythm compensates."*

—THE KYBALION.

The great Fifth Hermetic Principle—the Principle of
Rhythm—embodies the truth that in everything there
is manifested a measured motion; a to-and-from movement; a flow and inflow; a swing forward and backward;
a pendulum-like movement; a tide-like ebb and flow; a
high-tide and a low-tide; between the two-poles manifest
on the physical, mental or spiritual planes. The Principle
of rhythm is closely connected with the Principle of Polarity described in the preceding chapter. Rhythm manifests

between the two poles established by the Principle of Polarity. This does not mean, however, that the pendulum of Rhythm swings to the extreme poles, for this rarely happens; in fact, it is difficult to establish the extreme polar opposites in the majority of cases. But the swing is ever "toward" first one pole and then the other.

There is always an action and reaction; an advance and a retreat; a rising and a sinking; manifested in all of the airs and phenomena of the Universe. Suns, worlds, men, animals, plants, minerals, forces, energy, mind and matter, yes, even Spirit, manifests this Principle. The Principle manifests in the creation and destruction of worlds; in the rise and fall of nations; in the life history of all things; and finally in the mental states of Man.

Beginning with the manifestations of Spirit—of THE ALL—it will be noticed that there is ever the Outpouring and the Indrawing; the "Outbreathing and Inbreathing of Brahm," as the Brahmans word it. Universes are created; reach their extreme low point of materiality; and then begin in their upward swing. Suns spring into being, and then their height of power being reached, the process of retrogression begins, and after aeons they become dead masses of matter, awaiting another impulse which starts again their inner energies into activity and a new solar life cycle is begun. And thus it is with all the worlds; they are born, grow and die; only to be reborn. And thus it is with all the things of shape and form; they swing from action to reaction; from birth to death; from activity to inactivity—and then back again. Thus it is with all living things; they are born, grow, and die—and then are reborn. So it is with all great movements, philosophies, creeds, fashions, governments, nations, and all else—birth, growth, maturity, decadence, death—and then new-birth. The swing of the pendulum is ever in evidence.

Night follows day; and day night. The pendulum swings from Summer to Winter, and then back again. The corpuscles, atoms, molecules, and all masses of matter, swing around the circle of their nature. There is no such thing as absolute rest, or cessation from movement, and all movement partakes of rhythm. The principle is of universal application. It may be applied to any question, or phenomena of any of the many planes of life. It may be applied to all phases of human activity.

There is always the Rhythmic swing from one pole to the other. The Universal Pendulum is ever in motion. The Tides of Life flow in and out, according to Law.

The Principle of rhythm is well understood by modern science, and is considered a universal law as applied to material things. But the Hermetists carry the principle much further, and know that its manifestations and influence extend to the mental activities of Man, and that it accounts for the bewildering succession of moods, feelings and other annoying and perplexing changes that we notice in ourselves. But the Hermetists by studying the operations of this Principle have learned to escape some of its activities by Transmutation.

The Hermetic Masters long since discovered that while the Principle of Rhythm was invariable, and ever in evidence in mental phenomena, still there were two planes of its manifestation so far as mental phenomena are concerned. They discovered that there were two general planes of Consciousness, the Lower and the Higher, the understanding of which fact enabled them to rise to the higher plane and thus escape the swing of the Rhythmic pendulum which manifested on the lower plane. In other words, the swing of the pendulum occurred on the Unconscious Plane, and the Consciousness was not affected. This they call the Law of Neutralization. Its operations consist in the raising of the Ego above the vibrations of the Unconscious Plane of mental activity, so that the negative-swing of the pendulum is not manifested in consciousness, and therefore they are not affected. It is akin to rising above a thing and letting it pass beneath you. The Hermetic Master, or advanced student, polarizes himself at the desired pole, and by a process akin to "refusing" to participate in the backward swing or, if you prefer, a "denial" of its influence over him, he stands firm in his polarized position, and allows the mental pendulum to swing back along the unconscious plane. All individuals who have attained any degree of self-mastery, accomplish this, more or less unknowingly, and by refusing to allow their moods and negative mental states to affect them, they apply the Law of Neutralization. The Master, however, carries this to a much higher degree of proficiency, and by the use of his Will he attains a degree of Poise and Mental Firmness almost impossible of belief on the part of those who allow themselves to be swung backward and forward by the mental pendulum of moods and feelings.

The importance of this will be appreciated by any thinking person who realizes what creatures of moods, feelings and emotion the majority of people are, and how little mastery of themselves they manifest. If you will stop and consider a moment, you will realize how much these swings of Rhythm have affected you in your life—how a period of Enthusiasm has been invariably followed by an opposite feeling and mood of Depression. Likewise, your moods and periods of Courage have been succeeded by equal moods of Fear. And so it has ever been with the majority of persons—tides of feeling have ever risen and fallen with them, but they have never suspected the cause or reason of the mental phenomena. An understanding of the workings of this Principle will give one the key to the Mastery of these rhythmic swings of feeling, and will enable him to know himself better and to avoid being carried away by these inflows and outflows. The Will is superior to the conscious manifestation of this Principle, although the Principle itself can never be destroyed. We may escape its effects, but the Principle operates, nevertheless. The pendulum ever swings, although we may escape being carried along with it.

There are other features of the operation of this Principle of Rhythm of which we wish to speak at this point. There comes into its operations that which is known as the Law of Compensation. One of the definitions or meanings of the word "Compensate" is, "to counterbalance" which is the sense in which the Hermetists use the term. It is this Law of Compensation to which the Kybalion refers when it says: "The measure of the swing to the right is the measure of the swing to the left; rhythm compensates."

The Law of Compensation is that the swing in one direction determines the swing in the opposite direction, or to the opposite pole—the one balances, or counterbalances, the other. On the Physical Plane we see many examples of this Law. The pendulum of the clock swings a certain distance to the right, and then an equal distance to the left. The seasons balance each other in the same way. The tides follow the same Law. And the same Law is manifested in all the phenomena of Rhythm. The pendulum, with a short swing in one direction, has but a short swing in the other; while the long swing to the right invariably means the long swing to the left. An object hurled upward to a certain height has an equal distance to traverse on its return. The force with which a projectile is sent upward a mile is reproduced when the projectile returns to the earth on its return journey. This Law is constant on the Physical Plane, as reference to the standard authorities will show you.

But the Hermetists carry it still further. They teach that a man's mental states are subject to the same Law. The man who enjoys keenly, is subject to keen suffering; while he who feels but little pain is capable of feeling but little joy. The pig suffers but little mentally, and enjoys but little—he is compensated. And on the other hand, there are other animals who enjoy keenly, but whose nervous organism and temperament cause them to suffer exquisite degrees of pain and so it is with Man. There are temperaments which permit of but low degrees of enjoyment, and equally low degrees of suffering; while there are others which permit the most intense enjoyment, but also the most intense suffering. The rule is that the capacity for pain and pleasure, in each individual, are balanced. The Law of Compensation is in full operation here.

But the Hermetists go still further in this matter. They teach that before one is able to enjoy a certain degree of pleasure, he must have swung as far, proportionately, toward the other pole of feeling. They hold, however, that the Negative is precedent to the Positive in this matter, that is to say that in experiencing a certain degree of pleasure it does not follow that he will have to "pay up for it" with a corresponding degree of pain; on the contrary, the pleasure is the Rhythmic swing, according to the Law of Compensation, for a degree of pain previously experienced either in the present life, or in a previous incarnation. This throws a new light on the Problem of Pain.

The Hermetists regard the chain of lives as continuous, and as forming a part of one life of the individual, so that in consequence the rhythmic swing is understood in this way, while it would be without meaning unless the truth of reincarnation is admitted.

But the Hermetists claim that the Master or advanced student is able, to a great degree, to escape the swing toward Pain, by the process of Neutralization before mentioned. By rising on to the higher plane of the Ego, much of the experience that comes to those dwelling on the lower plane is avoided and escaped.

The Law of Compensation plays an important part in the lives of men and women. It will be noticed that one generally "pays the price" of anything he possesses or lacks. If he has one thing, he lacks another—the balance is struck. No one can "keep his penny and have the bit of cake" at the same time Everything has its pleasant and unpleasant sides. The things that one gains are always paid for by the things that one loses. The rich possess much that the poor lack, while the poor often possess things that are beyond the reach of the rich. The millionaire may have the inclination toward feasting, and the wealth wherewith to secure all the dainties and luxuries of the table, while he lacks the appetite to enjoy the same; he envies the appetite and digestion of the laborer who lacks the wealth and inclinations of the millionaire, and who gets more pleasure from his plain food than the millionaire could obtain even if his appetite were not jaded, nor his digestion ruined, for the wants, habits and inclinations differ. And so it is through life. The Law of Compensation is ever in operation, striving to balance and counter-balance, and always succeeding in time, even though several lives may be required for the return swing of the Pendulum of Rhythm.

COMMENTARY

The fifth principle is the *law of rhythm*, which relates closely to the principle of polarity. It is the idea that life is *pendulous* and circumstances inevitably and lawfully change on their scale.

Let's say you are feeling exuberant. Based on the law of rhythm, it is a fact of life that eventually, sometimes abruptly, the pendulum is going to swing from exuberance to ennui. But the principle of rhythm also holds that if you *observe* this phenomenon, if you become aware of it as it is happening, you can allow the pendulum swing to occur on a lesser or lower psychological plane, and you can, through an act of will, elevate your thoughts *so that you are observing but not taken by the pendulum swing*. This is how *The Kybalion* prescribes pitting one law against another.

The rhythms of emotion are ever present, they cannot be avoided, but they can be *observed*. Observe the pendulum swing within yourself, allow it to swing, don't try to fight it. It's a natural law, it must occur. You don't fight the wind. But if you observe it you can see it occurring on a lower scale of your psyche while you remain elevated and act the part of observer.

This is important for people who are deeply sensitive, who have what might be called an artistic temperament. The artist feels rhythmic changes keenly and intensely. That is part of what gives the artist empathy and insight. We sometimes call this mood swings, but I prefer not to use that term. This phenomenon aids creativity—but it can also be painful. The idea is not to get away from it, diagnose it, or fight it; the idea rather is to observe it. Higher spheres of life exist within you, just as within the physical universe, and from these spheres you can observe things and not feel the whole of yourself taken with the rhythmic swing.

Years ago following a week of a spiritual work in an isolated setting I prepared to return home. A colleague told me: "Your energy is going to drop. Don't drop with it."   —MH

Chapter 12

Causation

"Every Cause has its Effect; every Effect has its Cause; everything happens according to Law; Chance is but a name for Law not recognized; there are many planes of causation, but nothing escapes the Law."
—THE KYBALION.

The great Sixth Hermetic Principle—the Principle of Cause and Effect—embodies the truth that Law pervades the Universe; that nothing happens by Chance; that Chance is merely a term indicating cause existing but not recognized or perceived; that phenomena is continuous, without break or exception.

The Principle of Cause and Effect underlies all scientific thought, ancient and modern, and was enunciated by the Hermetic Teachers in the earliest days. While many and varied disputes between the many schools of thought have since arisen, these disputes have been principally upon the details of the operations of the Principle, and still more often upon the meaning of certain words. The underlying Principle of Cause and Effect has been accepted as correct by practically all the thinkers of the world worthy of the name. To think otherwise would be to take the phenomena of the universe from the domain of Law and Order, and to relegate it; to the control of the imaginary something which men have called "Chance."

A little consideration will show anyone that there is in reality no such thing as pure chance. Webster defines the word "Chance" as follows: "A supposed agent or mode of activity other than a force, law or purpose; the operation or activity of such agent; the supposed effect of such an agent; a happening; fortuity; casualty, etc." But a little consideration will show you that there can be no such agent as "Chance," in the sense of something outside of Law—something outside of Cause and Effect. How could there be a something acting in the phenomenal universe, independent of the laws, order, and continuity of the latter? Such a something would be entirely independent of the orderly trend of the universe, and therefore superior to it. We can imagine nothing outside of THE ALL being outside of the Law, and that only because THE ALL is the LAW in itself. There is no room in the universe for a something outside of and independent of Law. The existence of such a Something would render all Natural Laws ineffective, and would plunge the universe into chaotic disorder and lawlessness.

A careful examination will show that what we call "Chance" is merely an expression relating to obscure causes; causes that we cannot perceive; causes that we cannot understand. The word Chance is derived from a word Meaning "to fall" (as the falling of dice), the idea being that the fall of the dice (and many other happenings) are merely a "happening" unrelated to any cause. And this is the sense in which the term is generally employed. But when the matter is closely examined, it is seen that there is no chance whatsoever about the fall of the dice. Each time a die falls, and displays a certain number, it obeys a law as infallible as that which governs the revolution of the planets around the sun. Back of the fall of the die are causes, or chains of causes, running back further than the mind can follow. The position of the die in the box; the amount of muscular energy expended in the throw; the condition of the table, etc., etc., all are causes, the effect of which may be seen. But back of these seen causes there are chains of unseen preceding causes, all of which had a bearing upon the number of the die which fell uppermost.

If a die be cast a great number of times, it will be found that the numbers shown will be about equal, that is, there will be an equal number of one-spot, two-spot, etc., coming uppermost. Toss a penny in the air, and it may come down either "heads" or "tails"; but make a sufficient number of tosses, and the heads and tails will about even up.

This is the operation of the law of average. But both the average and the single toss come under the Law of Cause and Effect, and if we were able to examine into the preceding causes, it would be clearly seen that it was simply impossible for the die to fall other than it did, under the same circumstances and at the same time. Given the same causes, the same results will follow. There is always a "cause" and a "because" to every event. Nothing ever "happens" without a cause, or rather a chain of causes.

Some confusion has arisen in the minds of persons considering this Principle, from the fact that they were unable to explain how one thing could cause another thing—that is, be the "creator" of the second thing. As a matter of fact, no "thing" ever causes or "creates" another "thing." Cause and Effect deals merely with "events." An "event" is "that which comes, arrives or happens, as a result or consequent of some preceding event." No event "creates" another event, but is merely a preceding link in the great orderly chain of events flowing from the creative energy of THE ALL. There is a continuity between all events precedent, consequent and subsequent. There is a relation existing between everything that has gone before, and everything that follows. A stone is dislodged from a mountain side and crashes through a roof of a cottage in the valley below. At first sight we regard this as a chance effect, but when we examine the matter we find a great chain of causes behind it. In the first place there was the rain which softened the earth supporting the stone and which allowed it to fall; then back of that was the influence of the sun, other rains, etc., which gradually disintegrated the piece of rock from a larger piece; then there were the causes which led to the formation of the mountain, and its upheaval by convulsions of nature, and so on ad infinitum. Then we might follow up the causes behind the rain, etc.

Then we might consider the existence of the roof In short, we would soon find ourselves involved in a mesh of cause and effect, from which we would soon strive to extricate ourselves.

Just as a man has two parents, and four grandparents, and eight great-grandparents, and sixteen great-great-grandparents, and so on until when, say, forty generations are calculated the numbers of ancestors run into many millions—so it is with the number of causes behind even the most trifling event or phenomena, such as the passage of a tiny speck of soot before your eye. It is not an easy matter to trace the bit of soot hack to the early period of the world's history when it formed a part of a massive tree-trunk, which was afterward converted into coal, and so on, until as the speck of soot it now passes before your vision on its way to other adventures. And a mighty chain of events, causes and effects, brought it to its present condition, and the later is but one of the chain of events which will go to produce other events hundreds of years from now. One of the series of events arising from the tiny bit of soot was the writing of these lines, which caused the typesetter to perform certain work; the proofreader to do likewise; and which will arouse certain thoughts in your mind, and that of others, which in turn will affect others, and so on, and on, and on, beyond the ability of man to think further—and all from the passage of a tiny bit of soot, all of which shows the relativity and association of things, and the further fact that "there is no great; there is no small, in the mind that causeth all."

Stop to think a moment. If a certain man had not met a certain maid, away back in the dim period of the Stone Age—you who are now reading these lines would not now be here. And if, perhaps, the same couple had failed to meet, we who now write these lines would not now be here. And the very act of writing, on our part, and the act of reading, on yours, will affect not only the respective lives of yourself and ourselves, but will also have a direct, or indirect, affect upon many other people now living and who will live in the ages to come. Every thought we think, every act we perform, has its direct and indirect results which fit into the great chain of Cause and Effect.

We do not wish to enter into a consideration of Free Will, or Determinism, in this work, for various reasons. Among the many reasons, is the principal one that neither side of the controversy is entirely right—in fact, both sides are partially right, according to the Hermetic Teachings. The Principle of Polarity shows that both are but Half-Truths the opposing poles of Truth. The Teachings are that a man may be both Free and yet bound by

Necessity, depending upon the meaning of the terms, and the height of Truth from which the matter is examined. The ancient writers express the matter thus: "The further the creation is from the Centre, the more it is bound; the nearer the Centre it reaches, the nearer Free is it."

The majority of people are more or less the slaves of heredity, environment, etc., and manifest very little Freedom. They are swayed by the opinions, customs and thoughts of the outside world, and also by their emotions, feelings, moods, etc. They manifest no Mastery, worthy of the name. They indignantly repudiate this assertion, saying, "Why, I certainly am free to act and do as I please—I do just what I want to do," but they fail to explain whence arise the "want to" and "as I please." What makes them "want to" do one thing in preference to another; what makes them "please" to do this, and not do that? Is there no "because" to their "pleasing" and "Wanting"? The Master can change these "pleases" and "wants" into others at the opposite end of the mental pole. He is able to "Will to will," instead of to will because some feeling, mood, emotion, or environmental suggestion arouses a tendency or desire within him so to do.

The majority of people are carried along like the falling stone, obedient to environment, outside influences and internal moods, desires, etc., not to speak of the desires and wills of others stronger than themselves, heredity, environment, and suggestion, carrying them along without resistance on their part, or the exercise of the Will.

Moved like the pawns on the checkerboard of life, they play their parts and are laid aside after the game is over. But the Masters, knowing the rules of the game, rise above the plane of material life, and placing themselves in touch with the higher powers of their nature, dominate their own moods, characters, qualities, and polarity, as well as the environment surrounding them and thus become Movers in the game, instead of Pawns—Causes instead of Effects. The Masters do not escape the Causation of the higher planes, but fall in with the higher laws, and thus master circumstances on the lower plane. They thus form a conscious part of the Law, instead of being mere blind instruments. While they Serve on the Higher Planes, they Rule on the Material Plane.

But, on higher and on lower, the Law is always in operation. There is no such thing as Chance. The blind goddess has been abolished by Reason. We are able to see now, with eyes made clear by knowledge, that everything is governed by Universal Law—that the infinite number of laws are but manifestations of the One Great Law—the LAW which is THE ALL. It is true indeed that not a sparrow drops unnoticed by the Mind of THE ALL—that even the hairs on our head are numbered—as the scriptures have said There is nothing outside of Law; nothing that happens contrary to it. And yet, do not make the mistake of supposing that Man is but a blind automaton—far from that. The Hermetic Teachings are that Man may use Law to overcome laws, and that the higher will always prevail against the lower, until at last he has reached the stage in which he seeks refuge in the LAW itself, and laughs the phenomenal laws to scorn. Are you able to grasp the inner meaning of this?

COMMENTARY

Principle six is *cause and effect*. The idea behind this principle is that everything is lawful; everything has some antecedent or cause. Nothing just occurs. Symmetries rule life. If you flip a coin a certain number of times eventually heads and tails statistically even out. We may look upon such an occurrence and ask, "Well, so what?" But it's actually extraordinary because it demonstrates on the simplest level that there are lawful, necessary outcomes.

Practically speaking, it is not possible that if you flip a penny 10,000 times you'll come up with 10,000 heads or 10,000 tails. Nor is it possible that you will deviate more than a very few points from a 50-50 outcome. Why would that be? Why shouldn't you get 10,000 heads or 10,000 tails or 9,000 heads? If you were to get just 6,000 of one side out of 10,000 flips, the odds would be astronomically slender. A repeat occurrence would violate all known laws. You would then have to search for an unseen cause. It is not always easy to make that determination. It is not always possible.

Even this simple example demonstrates cause and effect at work behind circumstances.

The challenge is determining *what the cause and effect is*.

Sometimes a cause may involve a vast chain of events. Right now you are reading a book about Hermeticism. Myriad factors brought you to this place. Among them, perhaps, is that one of our ancient forebears may have been sitting in a temple in Alexandria and said, "We must write this down—ask Tat, he'll do it." Maybe that's among the chain of reasons why you're reading this today.

The principle of cause and effect holds that nothing is random. Nothing is coincidental. Nothing is purely accidental. Everything follows some network of events that makes the outcome possible, and in some cases makes it the only possible outcome.

The question is, do we have the perspective to discern the continuum, and to get involved in it if we wish? Sometimes we do. Sometimes you can use these laws to alter an outcome. Sometimes we lack the perspective, or the series of events are too vast. Perhaps we don't have all the information at hand. I'm awestruck at the paucity of facts I possess. Let's say I want to make a judgment about something or someone. Most of the time I am completely bereft of facts. I am just operating off of a script based upon things that I've previously done or thought, or based upon emotional reactions and conditioned responses. My script, if I stopped to consider it, is terrifyingly limited.

Almost all of my responses life seem to consist of about one of twenty things. We think of ourselves as free beings. Yet nearly everything I do comes down to one out of about twenty choices, with few facts bearing even upon those. Most of the time I am reading from a mental-emotional script that I've settled on based upon attitudes, traits, or warnings that were inculcated in me very early in life. It's almost as if I have a board with twenty sticky notes on it and I take one down: here's where I'm indignant; here's where I'm afraid; here's where I'm ingratiating.

We're filled with untapped possibilities; we live in a universe where everything has a vast range of cause and effect. Yet rather than seeking these facts, I just take down one of my sticky notes and react.

Again, there are times where cause and effect cannot be known because the facts are unavailable. But let's at least hold the question. Let's realize with this sixth Hermetic law that there *is* an orderly, if not always viewable, progression of events. If there is an orderly progression we can intervene in a multitude of ways. But it may not be given to us to see.

Let's at least hold the thought that usually we do not know the factors behind something. When we think we do, it's often a trap. The principle of cause and effect tells us that we do not know, but also that events are not accidental and they probably do not belong to the script I've reduced to sticky notes. Something greater is going on. What is it? Hold that question.   —MH

Chapter 13

Gender

"Gender is in everything; everything has its Masculine and Feminine Principles; Gender manifests on all planes."

—THE KYBALION.

The great Seventh Hermetic Principle—the Principle of Gender—embodies the truth that there is Gender manifested in everything—that the Masculine and Feminine principles are ever present and active in all phases of phenomena, on each and every plane of life. At this point we think it well to call your attention to the fact that Gender, in its Hermetic sense, and Sex in the ordinarily accepted use of the term, are not the same.

The word "Gender" is derived from the Latin root meaning "to beget; to procreate; to generate; to create; to produce." A moment's consideration will show you that the word has a much broader and more general meaning than the term "Sex," the latter referring to the physical distinctions between male and female living things. Sex is merely a manifestation of Gender on a certain plane of the Great Physical Plane—the plane of organic life. We wish to impress this distinction upon your minds, for the reason that certain writers, who have acquired a smattering of the Hermetic Philosophy, have sought to identify this Seventh Hermetic Principle with wild and fanciful, and often reprehensible, theories and teachings regarding Sex.

The office of Gender is solely that of creating, producing, generating, etc., and its manifestations are visible on every plane of phenomena. It is somewhat difficult to produce proofs of this along scientific lines, for the reason that science has not as yet recognized this Principle as of universal application. But still some proofs are forthcoming from scientific sources. In the first place, we find a distinct manifestation of the Principle of Gender among the corpuscles, ions, or electrons, which constitute the basis of Matter as science now knows the latter, and which by forming certain combinations form the Atom, which until lately was regarded as final and indivisible.

The latest word of science is that the atom is composed of a multitude of corpuscles, electrons, or ions (the various names being applied by different authorities) revolving around each other and vibrating at a high degree and intensity. But the accompanying statement is made that the formation of the atom is really due to the clustering of negative corpuscles around a positive one—the positive corpuscles seeming to exert a certain influence upon the negative corpuscles, causing the latter to assume certain combinations and thus "create" or "generate" an atom. This is in line with the most ancient Hermetic Teachings, which have always identified the Masculine principle of Gender with the "Positive," and the Feminine with the "Negative" Poles of Electricity (so called).

Now a word at this point regarding this identification. The public mind has formed an entirely errone-ous impression regarding the qualities of the so-called "Negative" pole of electrified or magnetized Matter. The terms Positive and Negative are very wrongly applied to this phenomenon by science. The word Positive means something real and strong, as compared with a Nega-tive unreality or weakness. Nothing is further from the real facts of electrical phenomenon. The so-called Nega-tive pole of the battery is really the pole in and by which the generation or production of new forms and energies is manifested. There is nothing "negative" about it. The best scientific authorities now use the word "Cathode" in place of "Negative," the word Cathode coming from the Greek root meaning "descent; the path of generation, etc," From the Cathode pole emerge the swarm of electrons or corpuscles; from the same pole emerge those wonderful "rays" which have revolutionized scientific conceptions during the past decade. The Cathode pole is the Mother of all of the strange phenomena which have rendered useless the old textbooks, and which have caused many long accepted theories to be relegated to the scrap-pile of scientific speculation. The Cathode, or Negative Pole, is the Mother Principle of Electrical Phenomena, and of the finest forms of matter as yet known to science. So you see we are justified in refusing to use the term "Negative" in our consideration of the subject, and in insisting upon substituting the word "Feminine" for the old term. The facts of the case bear us out in this, without taking the Hermetic Teachings into consideration. And so we shall use the word "Feminine" in the place of "Negative" in speaking of that pole of activity.

The latest scientific teachings are that the creative corpuscles or electrons are Feminine (science says "they are composed of negative electricity"—we say they are composed of Feminine energy).

A Feminine corpuscle becomes detached from, or rather leaves, a Masculine corpuscle, and starts on a new career. It actively seeks a union with a Masculine corpuscle, being urged thereto by the natural impulse to create new forms of Matter or Energy. One writer goes so far as to use the term "it at once seeks, of its own volition, a union," etc. This detachment and uniting form the basis of the greater part of the activities of the chemical world. When the Feminine corpuscle unites with a Masculine corpuscle, a certain process is begun. The Feminine particles vibrate rapidly under the influence of the Masculine energy, and circle rapidly around the latter. The result is the birth of a new atom. This new atom is really composed of a union of the Masculine and Feminine electrons, or corpuscles, but when the union is formed the atom is a separate thing, having certain properties, but no longer manifesting the property of free electricity. The process of detachment or separation of the Feminine electrons is called "ionization." These electrons, or corpuscles, are the most active workers in Nature's field. Arising from their unions, or combinations, manifest the varied phenomena of light, heat, electricity, magnetism, attraction, repulsion, chemical affinity and the reverse, and similar phenomena. And all this arises from the operation of the Principle of Gender on the plane of Energy.

The part of the Masculine principle seems to be that of directing a certain inherent energy toward the Feminine principle, and thus starting into activity the creative processes. But the Feminine principle is the one always doing the active creative work—and this is so on all planes. And yet, each principle is incapable of operative energy without the assistance of the other. In some of the forms of life, the two principles are combined in one organism. For that matter, everything in the organic world manifests both genders—there is always the Masculine present in the Feminine form, and the Feminine form. The Hermetic Teachings include much regarding the operation of the two principles of Gender in the production and manifestation of various forms of energy, etc., but we do not deem it expedient to go into detail regarding the same at this point, because we are unable to back up the same with scientific proof, for the reason that science has not as yet progressed thus far. But the example we have given you of the phenomena of the electrons or corpuscles will show you that science is on the right path, and will also give you a general idea of the underlying principles.

Some leading scientific investigators have announced their belief that in the formation of crystals there was to be found something that corresponded to "sex-activity" which is another straw showing the direction the scientific winds are blowing. And each year will bring other facts to corroborate the correctness of the Hermetic Principle of Gender. It will be found that Gender is in constant operation and manifestation in the field of inorganic matter, and in the field of Energy or Force. Electricity is now generally regarded as the "Something" into which all other forms of energy seem to melt or dissolve. The "Electrical Theory of the Universe" is the latest scientific doctrine, and is growing rapidly in popularity and general acceptance. And it thus follows that if we are able to discover in the phenomena of electricity—even at the very root and source of its manifestations a clear and unmistakable evidence of the presence of Gender and its activities, we are justified in asking you to believe that science at last has offered proofs of the existence in all universal phenomena of that great Hermetic Principle—the Principle of Gender.

It is not necessary to take up your time with the well known phenomena of the "attraction and repulsion" of the atoms; chemical affinity; the "loves and hates" of the atomic particles; the attraction or cohesion between the molecules of matter. These facts are too well known to need extended comment from us. But, have you ever considered that all of these things are manifestations of the Gender Principle? Can you not see that the phenomena is "on all fours" with that of the corpuscles or electrons? And more than this, can you not see the reasonableness of the Hermetic Teachings which assert that the very Law of Gravitation—that strange attraction by reason of which all particles and bodies of matter in the universe tend toward each other—is but another manifestation of the Principle of Gender, which operates in the direction of attracting the Masculine to the Feminine energies, and vice versa? We cannot offer you scientific proof of this at this time—but examine the phenomena in the light of the Hermetic Teachings on the subject, and see if you have not a better working hypothesis than any offered by physical science. Submit all physical phenomena to the test, and you will discern the Principle of Gender ever in evidence.

Let us now pass on to a consideration of the operation of the Principle on the Mental Plane. Many interesting features are there awaiting examination.

COMMENTARY

The seventh and final Hermetic principle is the *law of mental gender*. This means that nature, the cosmos, and everything in it have masculine and feminine sides.

The world stands on this principle: in all things there exists an intermingling of the masculine and the feminine, and a reconciling result.

The example that the author of *The Kybalion* uses in the following chapter, "Mental Gender," centers on the nature of the mind. You have a conscious mind, which is to say the analytic, logical mind. He called that the masculine principle. You have a subconscious mind, which is the mind that harbors images and memories, and gives birth to ideas. He called that the feminine principle. Each of us also has a will, which can observe and direct elements of the mind. Atkinson sees the will as a kind of life essence, which reflects The All. Just as The All as stands above all reality in the cosmos, the will in you stands above all other functions

Your will can direct the masculine principle—the functional, problem-solving mind—to transmit ideas, intentions, and notions to the subconscious, the feminine principle, which creates and gives birth.

You can picture things and create them on our scale of existence using the masculine and feminine nature of the mind. This phenomenon extends through the concentrically formed cosmos in which *all is mental.*

In every sphere of life, the mind creates using this formula: the conscious mind makes suggestions to the subconscious mind, which births the actualization. The reconciling force is result: the thing that you wish to create—and which you are capable of creating just as you have been created by The All.

These are the seven Hermetic principles as recorded in *The Kybalion.* Each of them is an amalgam of insights from Hermeticism, psychology, New Thought, and the sciences old and new, based upon and traceable to the Hermetica.

Since the following chapter and the one after repeat themes we have already explored, I will forego further commentary. Once you review those chapters I invite you to continue your exploration of Hermeticism in the afterword.   —MH

Chapter 14

Mental Gender

Students of psychology who have followed the modern trend of thought along the lines of mental phenomena are struck by the persistence of the dual-mind idea which has manifested itself so strongly during the past ten or fifteen years, and which has given rise to a number of plausible theories regarding the nature and constitution of these "two minds." The late Thomson J. Hudson attained great popularity in 1893 by advancing his well-known theory of the "objective and subjective minds" which he held existed in every individual. Other writers have attracted almost equal attention by the theories regarding the "conscious and subconscious minds"; the "voluntary and involuntary minds"; "the active and passive minds," etc., etc. The theories of the various writers differ from each other, but there remains the underlying principle of "the duality of mind."

The student of the Hermetic Philosophy is tempted to smile when he reads and hears of these many "new theories" regarding the duality of mind, each school adhering tenaciously to its own pet theories, and each claiming to have "discovered the truth." The student turns back the pages of occult history, and away back in the dim beginnings of occult teachings he finds references to the ancient Hermetic doctrine of the Principle of Gender on the Mental Plane—the manifestation of Mental Gender. And examining further he finds that the ancient philosophy took cognizance of the phenomenon of the "dual mind," and accounted for it by the theory of Mental Gender. This idea of Mental Gender may be explained in a few words to students who are familiar with the modern theories just alluded to. The Masculine Principle of Mind corresponds to the so-called Objective Mind; Conscious Mind; Voluntary Mind; Active Mind, etc. And the Feminine Principle of Mind corresponds to the so-called Subjective Mind; Sub-conscious Mind; Involuntary Mind; Passive Mind, etc. Of course the Hermetic Teachings do not agree with the many modern theories regarding the nature of the two phases of mind, nor does it admit many of the facts claimed for the two respective aspects—some of the said theories and claims being very far-fetched and incapable of standing the test of experiment and demonstration. We point to the phases of agreement merely for the purpose of helping the student to assimilate his previously acquired knowledge with the teachings of the Hermetic Philosophy. Students of Hudson will notice the statement at the beginning of his second chapter of "The Law of Psychic Phenomena," that: "The mystic jargon of the Hermetic philosophers discloses the same general idea"—i.e., the duality of mind. If Dr. Hudson had taken the time and trouble to decipher a little of "the mystic jargon of the Hermetic Philosophy," he might have received much light upon the subject of "the dual mind"—but then, perhaps, his most interesting work might not have been written. Let us now consider the Hermetic Teachings regarding Mental Gender.

The Hermetic Teachers impart their instruction regarding this subject by bidding their students examine the report of their consciousness regarding their Self. The students are bidden to turn their attention inward upon the Self dwelling within each. Each student is led to see that his consciousness gives him first a report of the existence of his Self—the report is "I Am." This at first seems to be the final words from the consciousness, but a little further examination discloses the fact that this "I Am" may be separated or split into two distinct parts, or aspects, which while working in unison and in conjunction, yet, nevertheless, may be separated in consciousness.

While at first there seems to be only an "I" existing, a more careful and closer examination reveals the fact that there exists an "I" and a "Me." These mental twins differ in their characteristics and nature, and an examination of their nature and the phenomena arising from the same will throw much light upon many of the problems of mental influence.

Let us begin with a consideration of the Me, which is usually mistaken for the I by the student, until he presses the inquiry a little further back into the recesses of consciousness. A man thinks of his Self (in its aspect of Me) as being composed of certain feelings, tastes likes, dislikes, habits, peculiar ties, characteristics, etc., all of which go to make up his personality, or the "Self" known to himself and others. He knows that these emotions and feelings change; are born and die away; are subject to the Principle of Rhythm, and the Principle of Polarity, which take him from one extreme of feeling to another. He also thinks of the "Me" as being certain knowledge gathered together in his mind, and thus forming a part of himself. This is the "Me" of a man.

But we have proceeded too hastily. The "Me" of many men may be said to consist largely of their consciousness of the body and their physical appetites, etc. Their consciousness being largely bound up with their bodily nature, they practically "live there." Some men even go so far as to regard their personal apparel as a part of their "Me" and actually seem to consider it a part of themselves. A writer has humorously said that "men consist of three parts—soul, body and clothes." These "clothes conscious" people would lose their personality if divested of their clothing by savages upon the occasion of a shipwreck. But even many who are not so closely bound up with the idea of personal raiment stick closely to the consciousness of their bodies being their "Me" They cannot conceive of a Self independent of the body. Their mind seems to them to be practically "a something belonging to" their body—which in many cases it is indeed.

But as man rises in the scale of consciousness he is able to disentangle his "Me" from his idea of body, and is able to think of his body as "belonging to" the mental part of him. But even then he is very apt to identify the "Me" entirely with the mental states, feelings, etc., which he feels to exist within him. He is very apt to consider these internal states as identical with himself, instead of their being simply "things" produced by some part of his mentality, and existing within him—of him, and in him, but still not "himself." He sees that he may change these internal states of feelings by all effort of will, and that he may produce a feeling or state of an exactly opposite nature, in the same way, and yet the same "Me" exists. And so after a while he is able to set aside these various mental states, emotions, feelings, habits, qualities, characteristics, and other personal mental belongings—he is able to set them aside in the "not-me" collection of curiosities and encumbrances, as well as valuable possessions. This requires much mental concentration and power of mental analysis on the part of the student. But still the task is possible for the advanced student, and even those not so far advanced are able to see, in the imagination, how the process may be performed.

After this laying-aside process has been performed, the student will find himself in conscious possession of a "Self" which may be considered in its "I" and "Me" dual aspects. The "Me" will be felt to be a Something mental in which thoughts, ideas, emotions, feelings, and other mental states may be produced. It may be considered as the "mental womb," as the ancients styled it—capable of generating mental offspring. It reports to the consciousness as a "Me" with latent powers of creation and generation of mental progeny of all sorts and kinds. Its powers of creative energy are felt to be enormous. But still it seems to be conscious that it must receive some form of energy from either its "I" companion, or else from some other "I" ere it is able to bring into being its mental creations. This consciousness brings with it a realization of an enormous capacity for mental work and creative ability.

But the student soon finds that this is not all that he finds within his inner consciousness. He finds that there exists a mental Something which is able to Will that the "Me" act along certain creative lines, and which is also able to stand aside and witness the mental creation. This part of himself he is taught to call his "I." He is able to rest in its consciousness at will. He finds there not a consciousness of an ability to generate and actively create, in the sense of the gradual process attendant upon mental operations, but rather a sense and consciousness of an ability to project an energy from the "I" to the "Me"—a process of "willing" that the mental creation begin and proceed. He also finds that the "I" is able to stand aside and witness the operations of the "Me's" mental creation and generation. There is this dual aspect in the mind of every person. The "I" represents the Masculine Principle of Mental Gender—the "Me" represents the Female Principle. The "I" represents the Aspect of Being; the "Me" the Aspect of Becoming. You will notice that the Principle of Correspondence operates on this plane just as it does upon the great plane upon which the creation of Universes is performed. The two are similar in kind, although vastly different in degree. "As above, so below; as below, so above."

These aspects of mind—the Masculine and Feminine Principles—the "I" and the "Me"—considered in connection with the well-known mental and psychic phenomena, give the master-key to these dimly known regions of mental operation and manifestation. The principle of Mental Gender gives the truth underlying the whole field of the phenomena of mental influence, etc.

The tendency of the Feminine Principle is always in the direction of receiving impressions, while the tendency of the Masculine Principle is always in the direction of giving, out or expressing. The Feminine Principle has much more varied field of operation than has the Masculine Principle. The Feminine Principle conducts the work of generating new thoughts, concepts, ideas, including the work of the imagination. The Masculine Principle contents itself with the work of the "Will" in its varied phases. And yet, without the active aid of the Will of the Masculine Principle, the Feminine Principle is apt to rest content with generating mental images which are the result of impressions received from outside, instead of producing original mental creations.

Persons who can give continued attention and thought to a subject actively employ both of the Mental Principles—the Feminine in the work of the mental generation, and the Masculine Will in stimulating and energizing the creative portion of the mind. The majority of persons really employ the Masculine Principle but little, and are content to live according to the thoughts and ideas instilled into the "Me" from the "I" of other minds. But it is not our purpose to dwell upon this phase of the subject, which may be studied from any good text-book upon psychology, with the key that we have given you regarding Mental Gender.

The student of Psychic Phenomena is aware of the wonderful phenomena classified under the head of Telepathy; Thought Transference; Mental Influence; Suggestion; Hypnotism, etc. Many have sought for an explanation of these varied phases of phenomena under the theories of the various "dual mind" teachers. And in a measure they are right, for there is clearly a manifestation of two distinct phases of mental activity. But if such students will consider these "dual minds" in the light of the Hermetic

Teachings regarding Vibrations and Mental Gender, they will see that the long sought for key is at hand.

In the phenomena of Telepathy it is seen how the Vibratory Energy of the Masculine Principle is projected toward the Feminine Principle of another person, and the latter takes the seed-thought and allows it to develop into maturity. In the same way Suggestion and Hypnotism operates. The Masculine Principle of the person giving the suggestions directs a stream of Vibratory Energy or Will-Power toward the Feminine Principle of the other person, and the latter accepting it makes it its own and acts and thinks accordingly. An idea thus lodged in the mind of another person grows and develops, and in time is regarded as the rightful mental offspring of the individual, whereas it is in reality like the cuckoo egg placed in the sparrows nest, where it destroys the rightful offspring and makes itself at home. The normal method is for the Masculine and Feminine Principles in a person's mind to co-ordinate and act harmoniously in conjunction with each other, but, unfortunately, the Masculine Principle in the average person is too lazy to act—the display of Will-Power is too slight—and the consequence is that such persons are ruled almost entirely by the minds and wills of other persons, whom they allow to do their thinking and willing for them. How few original thoughts or original actions are performed by the average person? Are not the majority of persons mere shadows and echoes of others having stronger wills or minds than themselves?

The trouble is that the average person dwells almost altogether in his "Me" consciousness and does not realize that he has such a thing as an "I." He is polarized in his Feminine Principle of Mind, and the Masculine Principle, in which is lodged the Will, is allowed to remain inactive and not employed.

The strong men and women of the world invariably manifest the Masculine Principle of Will, and their strength depends materially upon this fact. Instead of living upon the impressions made upon their minds by others, they dominate their own minds by their Will, obtaining the kind of mental images desired, and moreover dominate the minds of others likewise, in the same manner. Look at the strong people, how they manage to implant their seed-thoughts in the minds of the masses of the people, thus causing the latter to think thoughts in accordance with the desires and wills of the strong individuals. This is why the masses of people are such sheeplike creatures, never originating an idea of their own, nor using their own powers of mental activity.

The manifestation of Mental Gender may be noticed all around us in everyday life. The magnetic persons are those who are able to use the Masculine Principle in the way of impressing their ideas upon others. The actor who makes people weep or cry as he wills, is employing this principle. And so is the successful orator, statesman, preacher, writer or other people who are before the public attention. The peculiar influence exerted by some people over others is due to the manifestation of Mental Gender, along the Vibrational lines above indicated. In this principle lies the secret of personal magnetism, personal influence, fascination, etc., as well as the phenomena generally grouped under the name of Hypnotism.

The student who has familiarized himself with the phenomena generally spoken of as "psychic" will have discovered the important part played in the said phenomena by that force which science has styled "Suggestion," by which term is meant the process or method whereby an idea is transferred to, or "impressed upon" the mind of another, causing the second mind to act in accordance therewith. A correct understanding of Suggestion is necessary in order to intelligently comprehend the varied psychical phenomena which Suggestion underlies. But, still more is a knowledge of Vibration and Mental Gender necessary for the student of Suggestion. For the whole principle of Suggestion depends upon the principle of Mental Gender and Vibration.

It is customary for the writers and teachers of Suggestion to explain that it is the "objective or voluntary" mind which make the mental impression, or suggestion, upon the "subjective or involuntary" mind. But they do not describe the process or give us any analogy in nature whereby we may more readily comprehend the idea. But if you will think of the matter in the light of the Hermetic Teachings you will be able to see that the energizing of the Feminine Principle by the Vibratory Energy of the

Masculine Principle Is in accordance to the universal laws of nature, and that the natural world affords countless analogies whereby the principle may be understood. In fact, the Hermetic Teachings show that the very creation of the Universe follows the same law, and that in all creative manifestations, upon the planes of the spiritual, the mental, and the physical, there is always in operation this principle of Gender—this manifestation of the Masculine and the Feminine Principles. "As above, so below; as below, so above." And more than this, when the principle of Mental Gender is once grasped and understood, the varied phenomena of psychology at once becomes capable of intelligent classification and study, instead of being very much in the dark. The principle "works out" in practice, because it is based upon the immutable universal laws of life.

We shall not enter into an extended discussion of, or description of, the varied phenomena of mental influence or psychic activity. There are many books, many of them quite good, which have been written and published on this subject of late years. The main facts stated in these various books are correct, although the several writers have attempted to explain the phenomena by various pet theories of their own. The student may acquaint himself with these matters, and by using the theory of Mental Gender he will be able to bring order out of the chaos of conflicting theory and teachings, and may, moreover, readily make himself a master of the subject if he be so inclined. The purpose of this work is not to give an extended account of psychic phenomena but rather to give to the student a master-key whereby He may unlock the many doors leading into the parts of the Temple of Knowledge which he may wish to explore. We feel that in this consideration of the teachings of The Kybalion, one may find an explanation which will serve to clear away many perplexing difficulties—a key that will unlock many doors. What is the use of going into detail regarding all of the many features of psychic phenomena and mental science, provided we place in the hands of the student the means whereby he may acquaint himself fully regarding any phase of the subject which may interest him. With the aid of The Kybalion one may go through any occult library anew, the old Light from Egypt illuminating many dark pages, and obscure subjects. That is the purpose of this book. We do not come expounding a new philosophy, but rather furnishing the outlines of a great world-old teaching which will make clear the teachings of others—which will serve as a Great Reconciler of differing: theories, and opposing doctrines.

Chapter 15

Hermetic Axioms

"The possession of Knowledge, unless accompanied by a manifestation and expression in Action, is like the hoarding of precious metals—a vain and foolish thing. Knowledge, like wealth, is intended for Use. The Law of Use is Universal, and he who violates it suffers by reason of his conflict with natural forces."
—The Kybalion.

The Hermetic Teachings, while always having been kept securely locked up in the minds of the fortunate possessors thereof, for reasons which we have already stated, were never intended to be merely stored away and secreted. The Law of Use is dwelt upon in the Teachings, as you may see by reference to the above quotation from The Kybalion, which states it forcibly. Knowledge without Use and Expression is a vain thing, bringing no good to its possessor, or to the race. Beware of Mental Miserliness, and express into Action that which you have learned. Study the Axioms and Aphorisms, but practice them also.

We give below some of the more important Hermetic Axioms, from The Kybalion, with a few comments added to each. Make these your own, and practice and use them, for they are not really your own until you have Used them.

> "To change your mood or mental state—change your vibration." —THE KYBALION.

One may change his mental vibrations by an effort of Will, in the direction of deliberately fixing the Attention upon a more desirable state. Will directs the Attention, and Attention changes the Vibration. Cultivate the Art of Attention, by means of the Will, and you have solved the secret of the Mastery of Moods and Mental States.

> "To destroy an undesirable rate of mental vibration, put into operation the principle of Polarity and con-centrate upon the opposite pole to that which you de-sire to suppress. Kill out the undesirable by changing its polarity." —THE KYBALION.

This is one of the most important of the Hermetic For-mulas. It is based upon true scientific principles. We have shown you that a mental state and its opposite were merely the two poles of one thing, and that by Mental Transmutation the polarity might be reversed. This Principle is known to modern psychologists, who apply it to the breaking up of undesirable habits by bidding their students concentrate upon the opposite quality. If you are possessed of Fear, do not waste time trying to "kill out" Fear, but instead cultivate the quality of Courage, and the Fear will disappear. Some writers have expressed this idea most forcibly by using the illustration of the dark room. You do not have to shovel out or sweep out the Darkness, but by merely opening the shutters and letting in the Light the Darkness has disappeared. To kill out a Negative quality, concentrate upon the Positive Pole of that same quality, and the vibrations will gradually change from Negative to Positive, until finally you will become polarized on the Positive pole instead of the Negative. The reverse is also true, as many have found out to their sorrow, when they have allowed themselves to vibrate too constantly on the Negative pole of things. By changing your polarity you may master your moods, change your mental states, remake your disposition, and build up character. Much of the Mental Mastery of the advanced Hermetics is due to this application of Polarity, which is one of the important aspects of Mental Transmutation. Remember the Hermetic Axiom (quoted previously), which says:

> "*Mind (as well as metals and elements) may be transmuted from state to state; degree to degree, condition to condition; pole to pole; vibration to vibration.*"
>
> —THE KYBALION.

The mastery of Polarization is the mastery of the fundamental principles of Mental Transmutation or Mental Alchemy, for unless one acquires the art of changing his own polarity, he will be unable to affect his environment. An understanding of this principle will enable one to change his own Polarity, as well as that of others, if he will but devote the time, care, study and practice necessary to master the art. The principle is true, but the results obtained depend upon the persistent patience and practice of the student.

> "*Rhythm may be neutralized by an application of the Art of Polarization.*"   —THE KYBALION.

As we have explained in previous chapters, the Hermetists hold that the Principle of Rhythm manifests on the Mental Plane as well as on the Physical Plane, and that the bewildering succession of moods, feelings, emotions, and other mental states, are due to the backward and forward swing of the mental pendulum, which carries us from one extreme of feeling to the other.

The Hermetists also teach that the Law of Neutralization enables one, to a great extent, to overcome the operation of Rhythm in consciousness. As we have explained, there is a Higher Plane of Consciousness, as well as the ordinary Lower Plane, and the Master by rising mentally to the Higher Plane causes the swing of the mental pendulum to manifest on the Lower Plane, and he, dwelling on his Higher Plane, escapes the consciousness of the swing backward. This is effected by polarizing on the Higher Self, and thus raising the mental vibrations of the Ego above those of the ordinary plane of consciousness. It is akin to rising above a thing and allowing it to pass beneath you. The advanced Hermetist polarizes himself at the Positive Pole of his Being—the "I Am" pole rather than the pole of personality and by "refusing" and "denying" the operation of Rhythm, raises himself above its plane of consciousness, and standing firm in his Statement of Being he allows the pendulum to swing back on the Lower Plane without changing his Polarity. This is accomplished by all individuals who have attained any degree of self-mastery, whether they understand the law or not. Such persons simply "refuse" to allow themselves to be swung back by the pendulum of mood and emotion, and by steadfastly affirming the superiority they remain polarized on the Positive pole. The Master, of course, attains a far greater degree of proficiency, because he understands the law which he is overcoming by a higher law, and by the use of his Will he attains a degree of Poise and Mental Steadfastness almost impossible of belief on the part of those who allow themselves to be swung backward and forward by the mental pendulum of moods and feelings.

Remember always, however, that you do not really destroy the Principle of Rhythm, for that is indestructible. You simply overcome one law by counter-balancing it with another and thus maintain an equilibrium. The laws of balance and counter-balance are in operation on the mental as well as on the physical planes, and an understanding of these laws enables one to seem to overthrow laws, whereas he is merely exerting a counter-balance.

> *"Nothing escapes the Principle of Cause and Effect, but there are many Planes of Causation, and one may use the laws of the higher to overcome the laws of the lower."* —THE KYBALION.

By an understanding of the practice of Polarization, the Hermetists rise to a higher plane of Causation and thus counter-balance the laws of the lower planes of Causation. By rising above the plane of ordinary Causes they become themselves, in a degree, Causes instead of being merely Caused. By being able to master their own moods and feelings, and by being able to neutralize Rhythm, as we have already explained, they are able to escape a great part of the operations of Cause and Effect on the ordinary plane. The masses of people are carried along, obedient to their environment; the wills and desires of others stronger than themselves; the effects of inherited tendencies; the suggestions of those about them; and other outward causes; which tend to move them about on the chess-board of life like mere pawns. By rising above these influencing causes, the advanced Hermetists seek a higher plane of mental action, and by dominating their moods, emotions, impulses and feelings, they create for themselves new characters, qualities and powers, by which they overcome their ordinary environment, and thus become practically players instead of mere Pawns. Such people help to play the game of life understandingly, instead of being moved about this way and that way by stronger influences and powers and wills. They use the Principle of Cause and Effect, instead of being used by it. Of course, even the highest are subject to the Principle as it manifests on the higher planes, but on the lower planes of activity, they are Masters instead of Slaves. As The Kybalion says:

> "*The wise ones serve on the higher, but rule on the lower. They obey the laws coming from above them, But on their own plane, and those below them they rule and give orders. And, yet, in so doing, they form a part of the Principle, instead of opposing it. The wise man falls in with the Law, and by understanding its movements he operates it instead of being its blind slave. Just as does the skilled swimmer turn this way and that way, going and coming as he will, instead of being as the log which is carried here and there—so is the wise man as compared to the ordinary man— and yet both swimmer and log; wise man and fool, are subject to Law. He who understands this is well on the road to Mastery.*"   —THE KYBALION.

In conclusion let us again call your attention to the Hermetic Axiom:

"True Hermetic Transmutation is a Mental Art."

—THE KYBALION.

In the above axiom, the Hermetists teach that the great work of influencing one's environment is accomplished by Mental Power. The Universe being wholly mental, it follows that it may be ruled only by Mentality. And in this truth is to be found an explanation of all the phenomena and manifestations of the various mental powers which are attracting so much attention and study in these earlier years of the Twentieth Century. Back of and under the teachings of the various cults and schools, remains ever constant the Principle of the Mental Substance of the Universe. If the Universe be Mental in its substantial nature, then it follows that Mental Transmutation must change the conditions and phenomena of the Universe. If the Universe is Mental, then Mind must be the highest power affecting its phenomena. If this be understood then all the so-called "miracles" and "wonder-workings" are seen plainly for what they are.

"THE ALL is MIND; The Universe is Mental."

—THE KYBALION.

FINIS

Afterword

Your Journey into Hermeticism
by Mitch Horowitz

I encourage you to embark upon an independent study of the Hermetic literature I've been referencing, and to read that material hand in hand with *The Kybalion*.

In this afterword, I suggest some translations and starting points, as well as basic tracts that you'll want to cover. First I want to clarify some of the literary and historical terms that you encounter in the field of Hermeticism.

To start with, the term *Hermetica* is a catchall phrase used to describe the full range of late-ancient works considered part of the Hermetic tradition. The term *Corpus Hermeticum* refers primarily to the Hermetic tracts that were translated from Greek to Latin by Marsilio Ficino during the Renaissance.

Ficino's translation originally totaled fourteen tracts; these were later added to and subtracted from by other scholars so that we now have seventeen tracts tradition-ally called the *Corpus Hermeticum*. These works are often supplemented by a Latin Hermetic work called *Asclepius*, which was not part of Ficino's original but is among most beautiful and historically important tracts. Nor does the *Corpus* traditionally include the most famous Hermetic text called *The Emerald Tablet* ("as above, so below") since it emerged later and has only recently come to be recog-nized as authentic Hermetica.

If you study the table of contents of most translations of the *Corpus Hermeticum* you will discover that a "phan-tom tract"—number XV—is missing. This was a tenth-century A.D. work called the *Suda*, which ventured a more Christian interpretation of the figure of Hermes as a pagan who foresaw Christianity, a theme sounded by sev-eral early Christian writers. The *Suda* was later dubbed pseudo-Hermetica and removed. But tracts of the *Corpus Hermeticum* are still traditionally numbered one to eigh-teen, with the fifteenth entry absent.

Earlier I mentioned a paucity of good translations. Fortunately this problem is being redressed in our time by a crop of new translations. Two that I deeply admire and recommend are *Hermetica* translated by Brian P. Copenhaver (Cambridge University Press, 1992) and *The Way of Hermes* translated by Clement Salaman, Dorine van Oyen, William D. Wharton, and Jean-Pierre Mahe (Inner Traditions, 1999, 2000). I quote from both, and both are outstanding, but I must say a word of tribute to Copenhaver who not only launched the new wave of Hermetic translations but also wrote an invaluable historical introduction for his edition.

Other translations can be found online. Among the most historically valuable, and one almost certainly used by Atkinson himself, is G.R.S. Mead's *Thrice-Greatest Hermes*, a three-volume work of wide-ranging Hermetica published in 1906, two years before *The Kybalion*. Stylistically, Mead's translation is not one of my favorites. Mead was a beautiful scholar and an intellectual pioneer, but I find his translation marked by turgid, excessively formal Victorian prose. Nonetheless, it is serviceable and is considered textually accurate in ways that other period translations are not, including those by Walter Scott.

I should mention that there is a class of Hermetic writing sometimes called "technical Hermetica." It consists less of philosophy than of spells, alchemical operations, prayers, and rituals. Some of this material appears in Mead, but a much fuller selection can be found in *The Greek Magical Papyri in Translation* edited by Hans Dieter Betz (University of Chicago Press, 1986, 1992). Betz makes the important point that a great deal of technical Hermetica and other magical works got burned and destroyed by Christian inquisitors in antiquity and beyond.

* * *

In beginning your journey into Hermeticism, I recommend that you read three particular Hermetic books, which you can find in the above-referenced translations.

When I say "books" I should note that these passages are what we today would consider pamphlet-sized. They are brief, very powerful, and you will be able to see how each relates to the ideas in *The Kybalion*.

I recommend first reading book I of the *Corpus Hermeticum*, sometimes called *The Divine Pymander of Hermes Trismegistus*. Pymander is a Greek-Egyptian word thought to mean shepherd or shepherd of men. Other times the book is called *Poimandres*, which is a Hellenic variation. Ficino originally called his whole collection *Pymander*. Scholar of esotericism Richard Smoley points out that the term may be a Greek adaptation of the Egyptian p-eime-n-re or "mind of authority." Book I is profoundly dramatic and beautiful: Hermes Trismegistus encounters the Higher Mind, who teaches him about the individual's mirroring of the cosmos.

Next, I recommend book XI of the *Corpus Hermeticum*, which I consider perhaps the most important and influential of all extant Hermetic works. Book XI talks about the powers of mind and how the mind of the individual is imitative of the Higher Mind. Hermes is told that "nothing is impossible to you" through the powers of the mind; through the awakened mind the individual becomes like a god.

Finally, the third book that I encourage you to read is *Asclepius*. As mentioned, this is not part of the *Corpus Hermeticum* but it is usually included as a coda. It is not grouped with the *Corpus* because its original Greek source has never been found. *Asclepius* reached us only in Latin, but there exist Greek fragments of it. Hence, it is considered of the same vintage as the other Hermetic books. It is an achingly beautiful dialogue, and it may make you cry because offers a wistful (and accurate) prophecy of Ancient Egypt's decline. The epigraph of my first book *Occult America* is taken from *Asclepius*: "Oh, Egypt, Egypt, there will remain of they religion only fables . . ." Embedded within that prophecy, however, is a promise of the revival of the ancient gods.

I wish for you to read widely in Hermeticism but these are essentials and key starting points.

I now conclude this study guide on a personal note. I realize that, at times, all this talk of employing the agencies of the mind can seem frustrating when we feel crushed by the difficulties of life. There are times when all of us feel defeated by personal crisis, emotional pain, depression, disappointment, or sorrow. When physical or emotional pain, loss, grief, or just the burdens of daily existence have us in a grip, what should we do from the perspective of Hermetic wisdom?

Well, we talked about the law of rhythm. You can rely on the fact that there will be a pendulum swing. There may be times when that pendulum swing seems very far off. At 4 a.m. when you cannot sleep talk of pendulum swings is not a very warming sensation. In that regard, I feel strongly that appeals can be made to greater forces. I believe that prayer and petitions to a higher mind or entity represent a real and potent possibility. That, too, is a facet of Hermeticism. Prayer is historically part of the Hermetic experience.

In that vein, I invite you to ask with me: What if the ancient Hermeticists were correct? They were right about many things. What if when they encountered ancient Egypt's god of wisdom, Thoth, and fell to their knees, they had authentic insight? I am unprepared to say they did not.

What if you could make a direct appeal to Thoth Hermes Trismegistus? People pray all the time. Ours is a praying culture. What if? What if the ancient gods have been neglected—and hunger for your attention? What if they long for your veneration in a world that has forgotten them?

Read *Asclepius*, the beautiful, bittersweet dialogue that accurately prophesied the decline of Egypt and its pantheon. What if by reaching out to the gods, you find yourself in the position of giving hallowed comfort to an ancient entity or energy? Recall this passage from *Asclepius*: "He not only advances toward god; he also makes the gods strong."

Is there any rule that we must put only a certain name or names on the greater forces? Not for me. I suspect not for most of you reading these words.

I propose that you settle into a quiet or meditative mood tonight with these principles in mind. Return to the thought that I asked you to form at the beginning of this book—do you remember it?—and make a direct appeal to Hermes or Thoth. See what happens. Try it as a personal experiment. You're reading this volume because you're interested in spiritual philosophy.

Now, if what I am describing sounds foolish to you, don't do it. Don't waste your time.

But I am a seeker. And, as such, who am I to conclude that the Ancient Egyptians, whose empire existed for thousands of years—for centuries longer than what we call Western civilization—were wrong? When Greek historian Herodotus (484–425 BC) encountered the pyramids, the pyramids were as ancient to him as he is to us. Who am I to say that this empire had a misconception of greater forces?

Maybe the old gods are lonely. We've been withholding veneration for centuries, perhaps. This is just an experiment. You don't have to join anything. You don't have to tell anybody. They'll probably think you're crazy anyway, so it's better not to. But if you're moved by this idea, and if you take seriously the notion of a personal search, then along with what we've been considering, make a plea to the ancients. *Asclepius* not only prophesizes the Hermetic world's decline but also its rebirth.

I end this book on that note of hope—and with a wish for your highest fulfillment and development.

The Seeker Is the Master Key

About the Authors

"Three Initiates" is one of several pseudonyms used by WILLIAM WALKER ATKINSON, a popular and innovative New Thought writer and publisher in the early twentieth century. Born in Baltimore, Maryland, in 1862, Atkinson became a successful attorney in 1894. Following a series of illnesses, he immersed himself in New Thought literature. He soon became an important figure in the early days of the movement, publishing magazines such as *Suggestion, New Thought*, and *Advanced Thought*. Under the aegis of his own publishing company, Yogi Publication Society, Atkinson authored many bylined works and many titles written under the pseudonyms Yogi Ramacharaka, Magus Incognito, and Theron Q. Dumont. *The Kybalion* is the most popular and enduring work published by Atkinson's Chicago-based publishing house, and is perhaps the most widely read occult work of the twentieth century. Atkinson died in California in 1932.

MITCH HOROWITZ is one of today's most literate voices of esoterica and alternative spirituality. *The Washington Post* writes that Mitch "treats esoteric ideas and movements with an even-handed intellectual studiousness that is too often lost in today's raised-voice discussions." Mitch is the PEN Award-winning author of books including *Occult America*, *One Simple Idea*, *The Miracle Club*, *Secrets of Self-Mastery*, and *The Miracle Habits*. He received the Walden Award for Interfaith/Intercultural Understanding. The Chinese government has censored his work. Visit him on Twitter @MitchHorowitz and on Instagram @MitchHorowitz23.